ALSO BY DAMON YOUNG

What Doesn't Kill You Makes You Blacker

That's How
They Get You

That's How They Get You

✴

An Unruly Anthology
of Black American Humor

✴

Edited by

DAMON YOUNG

PANTHEON BOOKS
New York

FIRST EDITION PUBLISHED BY PANTHEON BOOKS 2025

Published by Pantheon Books, a division of Penguin Random House LLC,
1745 Broadway, New York, NY 10019.

Library of Congress Cataloging-in-Publication Data
Names: Young, Damon, 1978– editor.
Title: That's how they get you :
an anthology of new Black humor / edited by Damon Young.
Description: New York : Pantheon Books, 2025.
Identifiers: LCCN 2024043841 (print) | LCCN 2024043842 (ebook) |
ISBN 9780593317112 (hardcover) | ISBN 9780593317129 (ebook)
Subjects: LCSH: African American wit and humor. | LCGFT: Humor.
Classification: LCC PN6231.N5 T53 2025 (print) |
LCC PN6231.N5 (ebook) | DDC 818/.60208—dc23/eng/20241217
LC record available at https://lccn.loc.gov/2024043841
LC ebook record available at https://lccn.loc.gov/2024043842

penguinrandomhouse.com | pantheonbooks.com

Printed in the United States of America
2 4 6 8 9 7 5 3 1

The authorized representative in the EU for product safety and compliance
is Penguin Random House Ireland, Morrison Chambers, 32 Nassau Street,
Dublin D02 YH68, Ireland, https://eu-contact.penguin.ie.

To D.N.

Contents

Introduction:
Black Humor Is Every Brow

DAMON YOUNG

But for real I was already convinced, before that night in the back of the Kingsley's van, when Var Butler called Lumpy Moses an "instant-oatmeal Crip," that Var was the funniest person I'd ever met. Didn't realize until much later that he was a genius too.

Lump was just like the rest of us on the Kingsley Association's thirteen-and-under fall league hoop team. But then one day—and it felt like it happened in *just one day,* like Lump was a weekend guest on *Extreme Crippin' Makeover*—all his clothes were blue. His Champion sweats and Air Maxes were replaced by Dickies and Chucks. And every third word out his mouth was "cuz."

Gangs had begun to spread in the city, and there were dozens of Lumpys—Black boys still into Now and Laters and *Ren & Stimpy* who'd joined gangs like how rich white women join Goop. Like there was a trial subscription for crippin'. We didn't have the space for the perspective then that would've allowed us to see the grift of being fashionably Crip. Well, most of us didn't see it. Var somehow did.

I forget how it started. But I know we were on the Kingsley's van, headed to a game at Trees Hall on Pitt's campus. And Lumpy—who, despite his heavy crippin', still found time in his schedule to be the foul-prone eighth man on a rec center hoop team—was talking shit about snitches or starched slacks or whatever. Var had had enough.

> VAR: Nigga, *stop.*
> LUMPY: Huh?
> VAR: You ain't no Crip!
> LUMPY: Nigga, I'll—
> VAR: You'll do what? Everyone know you a instant-oatmeal Crip.
>   Like someone added water to your ass and boom!—instant
>   Crip. Go get some toast, my nigga.

Var killed Lump that day. Not literally, I mean. He's still alive. I actually saw him on a dip machine at LA Fitness last fall. He had good form. But Lumpy was no longer Lumpy. From that moment, until he moved with his babymom to Sacramento at twenty-two and came back to the Burgh without her at twenty-eight, his name was Oatmeal.

Var also saved his life. Because Oatmeal quit gangs a month later. He said he quit the Crips because he wanted to focus on ball. But he was already fourteen coming off the bench on a thirteen-and-under rec league team. Short and slow with great confidence and bad hands, he hooped like a microdosing penguin. His game was trash and never got better. Nah. He quit crippin' because Var shamed him out of it.

Var's comedic talents weren't limited to convincing half-assed Crips to go Rollerblade instead. He also intuitively knew the power dynamics baked into humor, where it's not just unkind to exclusively target people with less privilege than you; it makes your humor disposable and punchless. He was known from Homewood to the Hill for being the one nigga you ain't want a roasting session with. But he never went at people much younger or less popular than he was. He'd even bully the bullies, like the time on the bleachers at Pennley, when Reg Barlow was clowning Dev Hargrove for being so poor that he could only afford to eat bite-size Snickers for Thanksgiving dinner. Var jumped in, and by the time he was done with Reg, Reg was so furious and hysterical that he sulked home and came back with a screwdriver. (Var had already left, so Reg just went to McDonald's.) Var was also vaguely feminist. What else would you call a fourteen-year-old conscientious enough to call Robby Fields "fucking lame" for calling Brittini Wheeler a ho since Rob was just mad Brittini was going with E Rizzo? "So she a ho 'cause she don't wanna fuck with your ugly ass?" Var continued. "What kinda crackhead sense that make?"

What I didn't see then and didn't really realize until now was that Var had all the shit—all the sensibilities, all the stream-of-consciousness lucidities, all the observational anxieties, all the ways of distilling complexities to pithy and prescient one-liners—associated with what America considers its sharpest comedy. That's *Curb* and *Seinfeld* and *Veep*. That's Larry. That's Jerry. That's Tina. That's Woody. That's Louis. That's Wes. That's Mel. That's Judd. That's Joan. And the ingredient distinguishing this humor from the rest is neurosis—a brain so overstimulated and hyperactive that it just can't keep itself from experiencing excessive angst; from the vocalized awareness of a self-consciousness so deep it becomes vanity; from possessing and being known for peculiarities and idiosyncrasies so distinct and so settled that instead of you adjusting to the world, the world just must find a way to adjust to you. The possession of this sort of neurosis is assumed, by mainstream[*] critics and cultural tastemakers, to be a white-people thing. A *rich*-white-person thing. Because who else has the intellect, the time, and the opportunity to be *particular*? To possess angst? To carry an existential dread about manners? To be an introvert? To be crippled by and find levity in mild discomfort?

This assumption is goofy as fuck. Racist, sure. But mostly goofy. And *dumb*. But I fell victim to it too. I grew up watching and reading and listening to all the funny shit my parents allowed access to. *Mad* magazine. *In Living Color.* Hour-long HBO specials from Andrew Dice Clay and the half-hour bits from Paula Poundstone, Gilbert Gottfried, and Ellen DeGeneres. *Catch-22.* Dick Gregory. BET's *Comic View. The Golden Girls.* Bernie Mac. *High Anxiety.* SNL. *I'm Gonna Git You Sucka.* Robin Harris. *The Kids in the Hall.* But while Black comedians—particularly the holy triumvirate of Richard, Eddie, and Chris—were who made me laugh the hardest and the deepest, and

[*] White.

who shared the sort of shit that entered me as jokes and stayed there as both a politic and an analgesic, I still remember being an eighteen-year-old at Canisius College in 1997. And wanting to show the girls who came to my dorm room in Bosch Hall that I wasn't the average hoop nigga from the hood. And thinking that a prominently displayed *Seinfeld* VHS box set would evidence my wit better than *Def Comedy Jam* would. (I didn't have sex in that room my entire freshman year, though, so maybe the evidence was theoretical. Or maybe I needed to be funny myself instead of just brandishing funny shit, which was like curating a porn collection to prove you can fuck.)

I'd forgotten where I came from. Well maybe I didn't forget it as much as I just didn't want to remember it. Didn't want to acknowledge what walking through those same gang-infested Pittsburgh streets that made penguin-handed Oatmeal pretend he was O-Dog from *Menace* did to me. Did to us. Garfield, for instance, borders East Liberty (where I lived) to the west and was for the Bloods. East Lib itself was mostly neutral, except for the stretch closest to Larimer, which belonged to the Lincoln Avenue and Wilkinsburg (LAW) gang, who donned all black. Farther east was the Crip nexus of Lincoln/Lemington and Homewood. And to the east of Homewood was Wilkinsburg, which also belonged to the LAW. If this sounds confusing as fuck, that's because it *was*. The gangs gerrymandered the hood.

There were no clear demarcations either. No billboards announcing WELCOME TO HOMEWOOD: HOME OF WADE'S BARBER SHOP, THE GEORGE WESTINGHOUSE HIGH SCHOOL BULLDOGS, AND LIKE 127 CRIP NIGGAS. You could easily assume you were in Blood territory, cross a street, and get ice-grilled (or worse) by someone whose head-to-toe LA Dodgers fit ain't have shit to do with Hideo Nomo. (I'll never forget the time this Crip nigga in a Dodgers fitted rolled up to me and my homie Brian while we were hooping at Mellon Park. They knew each other, so Brian said, "What's up, killa?" They gave each other a quick pound, and the Crip nigga went to the other hoop and started shooting. When he was out of earshot, I turned to Brian. "Killa? He be killing niggas on the court? He got game like that?" Brian: "Nah. He killed someone.")

But while that time was scary and deadly and all that shit, it was also a refinement school for comedic genius. Who'd be more neurotic than a teenager who had to learn, overnight, how to navigate those streets? Who'd be more hypercognizant of manners and mannerisms, of body language and facial tics, of self-consciousnesses and vulnerabilities, of the importance of performance and punctuation? Whose observations would be more keen? Who'd be more adept at weaponizing humor and then, if necessary, repurposing it as an alleviator?

We didn't need this terror to be funny. Don't matter if you from Birmingham or Baltimore or Bel-Air. Existing while Black in America provides enough material. Generates enough anxiety. Produces enough demand for microbursts of levity. Places enough punch lines in plain view sometimes, and other times keeps them hidden and hazardous like fault lines. Requires enough catharsis and secret community, where truths are transmitted at frequencies so low they slip under your feet and enter your soul through your soles. Necessitates enough radical truth—an honesty that exists because the luxury of obliviousness just don't. An honesty that realizes, eventually, that obliviousness ain't a luxury. An honesty that realizes, eventually, that obliviousness is a crutch. An honesty that realizes, eventually, that the honesty necessary to exist while Black in America is a freedom. That we're not bound by the bazaar of lies that some Americans require to breathe and to think and to sit and to shit. That this bloody and Black-as-fuck honesty is where the best comedy is born. It's lowbrow. It's midbrow. It's highbrow. It's every brow.

Var's murder of Oatmeal was just as layered. The setting and the language gave it a lowbrow veneer. But his joke synthesized our collective exasperation over the prevalence of gangs with a queasiness about Oatmeal's cripping that we all *felt* but couldn't quite articulate, and then made a pitch-perfect analogy about hot cereal packets. Var finished the fatality with "Go get some toast, my nigga"—a kicker that reminded Oatmeal and everyone else on that bus that we knew each other too well to be that full of shit. Here, *nigga*—the English language's best Swiss Army knife—was a cold shower, a lie detector, and an antibiotic.

It's been over thirty years since that night, but I still remember it like it was yesterday. I remember how the rest of the team reacted after "Go get some toast, my nigga." It wasn't laughs but gasps, followed by the stunned silence that enters the atmosphere before the laughter removes the oxygen from it. Which is what happens when something is transcendently funny. It sticks to you. Sticks inside of you. Merges with you. It doesn't just tickle your funny bone. It smothers it. Incinerates it.

It's the same heat I felt that February night in 2004 after I'd just watched (pre–preoccupied-with-trans-people) Dave Chappelle's Prince catch lobs on Charlie Murphy's grill and then serve him pancakes, purified by the waters of Lake Minnetonka. It felt like my body and my brain were combusting. Like I'd just witnessed Chappelle conjure an event horizon and pull a skit out of it.

The Prince skit—a product of the Murphy-narrated "True Hollywood Stories" series on season two of *Chappelle's Show*—aired a week after the equally iconic Rick James bit, and that heat I felt was nuclear fusion. The realization that I'd just been reduced to ashes by a grade of humor I hadn't thought possible, and the collision between that feeling and a primal anticipation. What the fuck was he going to do *next week*?

He'd done the impossible the week before, somehow fusing oral history with surreality with impersonation with slapstick with memory with documentary with *five* catchphrases ("I'm Rick James, bitch," "Fuck your couch," "Darkness is spreading," "Cocaine is a hell of a drug," "They should've never gave y'all niggas money") with violence with Charlie Murphy's comedic timing and intonation with slow-motion instant replay with sight gags with *an actual character arc* for Dave Chappelle's Rick James in eight minutes of choreographed bedlam. It shouldn't have worked. But it did because of the juxtaposition of Murphy's hood everyman steez with Chappelle's absurdist depiction of James's untethered otherworldliness. And also because it was Black as fuck.

What makes Black humor *Black* ain't the subject matter, because not all humor involving Black people is Black. Sometimes it's just humor. Sometimes it's just Will Smith in *Hitch*. What makes it Black is exclusivity. If it only works because we're involved, and if the presence of Blackness grants it a freedom to go places no one else would. Or could.

The best humor is constructed around a surprise-wrapped truth-like substance. Whether it's actually true doesn't matter as much as the feeling of truth. Punch lines work the way jump scares do—the same language, the same rhythms, the same beats. You can't see them coming, because that would ruin it. But you *know* they're coming. You're waiting. They're there. They're *here*. And the best ones beat you the fuck up. You leave "in tears" or "in stitches." You "crack up." It has you "rollin'." Sometimes even "dead." You laugh your ass off, which means that you found a thing so funny that your whole entire booty kamikaze'd off your back. That's what Black humor—the best humor—does to you. It swallows air. It smothers bones. It cracks foreheads. It breaks brains. It extracts truth. It's messy. It's silly. It's searing. It's sticky. It's stank. It's diametrically unfettered by respectability, a spectrum stretching from Samantha Irby's transgressive vulnerability to Percival Everett's searing critique of the performance of race.

In *That's How They Get You,* it's meditations on love and grief and the function of humor from Hanif Abdurraqib, Ashon Crawley, Brian Broome, Ladan Osman, and Shamira Ibrahim. It's first-person recollections from Alexander Hardy, Clover Hope, Wyatt Cenac, and Roy Wood Jr. on navigating the terror of being a fish out of water. It's Nicola Yoon's and D Watkins's distinct perspectives on the circus of America-induced neuroses that come with raising a Black child here, and Angela Nissel's experience as a Black kid in this triflin' bedlam. It's Hillary Crosley Coker somehow finding levity in unspeakable trauma, Mahogany L. Browne's reminder of the beauty and necessity of a hype woman, and Jill Louise Busby on the disconcerting thrills of parasocial relationships. It's a conversation between Panama Jackson, Saida Grundy, and me on uncanny racial ironies. It's absurd farce from Mateo Askaripour, Rion Scott, and Joseph Earl Thomas. It's Deesha Philyaw on too much information from the worst possible source. And it's Nafissa Thompson-Spires taking us to school, Michael Harriot taking us to church, and Kiese Laymon taking us to shit.

It transcends format and form. This anthology includes fiction and nonfiction, autofiction and parody. Short story and memoir. Fabricated email exchanges and real actual text messages. There are gorillas and Karens in here. Pancake recipes and presumably safe urinals. Deaths and divorces. "Good" teeth and bad sex. Multiple biracials (well, like three) and several hood niggas. Sex workers and speed daters. Niggas with big booties and bitch-ass niggas. But mostly this book is a reminder. To leave shame behind. To leave respectability behind. To leave the performance of what I believed would communicate intellect behind. And to take Var with me everywhere I go now. To take the Kingsley van with me everywhere I go now. To take East Lib with me everywhere I go now. Because I think a part of me will always be that kid trying to impress girls in his dorm room. Only now I have that good shit.

That's How
They Get You

No One Makes "Yo Mama" Jokes
After the Funeral

HANIF ABDURRAQIB

Which is its own kind of joke. I don't make the rules about the decorum of the dozens, but I got good at the dozens because I knew I didn't want to fight. I could have fought, probably. I was the youngest of four, with two aggressive older brothers, and so I got my ass kicked plenty, and through a series of ass-whuppins, one learns how to at least hold one's own. At least survive. At least not get beaten up in front of a crowd. And jokes could delay the physical interaction if an eager enough audience was present. I got good at disarming a fist before it detonated. Though I wasn't entirely opposed to violence. There's an intimacy in the moment before a fight unfolds that I look back on now and find entirely romantic. Two people, circling each other, face-to-face, trying to—through that close looking—gauge each other's interest in limits and limitations, in line-crossing. Neither of them, given the day, all that particularly interested in fighting, but perhaps interested in seeing which of them might throw the first punch. The punch, too, another type of invitation for intimacy, for what doors it might open, how it might send two people tumbling to the ground, in each other's grasp.

But make no mistake, the dozens, too, is a performance of the intimate. All the best trash talkers I knew did their research, knew how exactly to hurt someone but not incite rage. To push someone to the point of being wounded enough to relent. The thing with the dozens is, one must get on a roll. It's like anything else. You respond to what the audience wants. If you get off a run of jokes and the audience is laughing with enough volume and ferocity, it almost doesn't matter what you're actually saying. Just the sound of your voice, performed with enough comedic melody, makes people believe that what is being said is already building atop the existing monument of jokes.

I got good at the dozens, too, explicitly because I had very little interest in hurting people. I had a code, even as a reckless and barely thoughtful adolescent. I stayed away from parents, from siblings. I could do twenty minutes on just one pair of busted-ass kicks I saw you wearing one time. Even if you didn't have them on at the time you became my target, I could summon them, make people believe you were wearing them.

But I was also a good sport. When people joked about my mother, her small stature, her hijab, the gap between her teeth, I didn't react to it in any way that would escalate the scene. The way I saw it, no one present in the dozens circle or on the school bus or in the locker bays knew my mother intimately, and so it was a waste of a joke. Like shouting at a ghost that only you and one other person can see.

And speaking of ghosts, I am at the point in my life where I have lived far longer without my mother than I have with her. At the point where, some days, I can't remember her voice as much as I can remember the sound of her laugh. Which was loud, which rattled walls and arrived in rooms several seconds before she did. She was a loud woman, despite being under five feet tall. Walked with volume, spoke with volume, in joy and in rage. A woman of immense volume. What I remember most from the months after she died was getting used to the silence. Even as a teenager, I lived a life defined by the sounds that furnished my life. When the lovingly loud person makes an exit, the silence is where the grief does its best living. When something was funny on the television and my family would laugh, there would be an absence. There was an absence of feet tumbling down the stairs, of belongings and grocery bags being thrown to the ground upon crossing the threshold of the home.

My mother died in the summer before my ninth-grade year, in a time when news spread around a neighborhood, and then spread to a school, and then spread, slowly, through a whole city. High school is a place of becoming, and I arrived fully formed in the minds of many. I was the kid with the dead mom, and that was my existence.

What happened first on the block, and then in the lunchrooms and the hallways where the dozens got played, was that the jokes would escalate, as they often did, and then someone would reach for the mother, the way you wind up before throwing what you believe to be a knockout punch. But then there would be a whisper, someone informing my opponent of the news. Their face would fall a bit, and they would stumble toward another, less potent joke.

In a way, this was how I first came to understand mercy, though it was a mercy I found myself despising. In my home, I was fine with being defined by absence, but in the world, beyond my house, I wanted to fight through it, to be a target beyond my grief.

The first time I encountered someone who didn't know that my mother had died and wasn't exactly concerned with the mechanics of grief, they offered up a "yo mama" joke that was so mundane, I can barely remember it. Something about how ugly she was, even though this person had never seen her. He got the joke out so quickly, it couldn't be stopped. There was a pause, a collective gasp, among the spectators. When he realized what he'd done, after someone shouted out, "She's dead, man, come on," he paused, became tentative, slightly sad and guarded, expecting me to snap, throw a punch.

What I remember is the unclenching of my fist. And, through the shocked silence, I threw my head back and laughed, loud. Not at the joke, but at the breaking down of an impossible wall, the freedom on the other side. My mother, sung back to life in a chamber of intimacy.

(My laughter caught my opponent off guard, which was the perfect time for me to rebound, swooping in to clown his busted-ass British Knights.)

The Couple

JILL LOUISE BUSBY

've followed them on Instagram—the married couple—for almost seven years. They've each followed me back for almost six years, and according to the bylaws of social media, that officially makes us friends.

Well, social media friends, at least.

But we're not just friends on social media. We're *almost* friends in real life, too. Because one time when I was in LA, I was supposed to DM the one I'd had more interaction with and let her know if I had time to hang out. She sent me her number and everything. And even though I never got around to saving it in my phone, I *have* it, you know? I know where it is should I ever need to use it. Should I ever find myself in LA with some time to finally meet and meet up. Should I ever make a move to merge the two worlds, snap the photo to prove that we're both real.

We didn't hang out that time, but we still could. As long as we still can, we're still almost friends. Admittedly, it's a newer kind of closeness. The kind that's formed at a distance, through a filter, on a social app that is aging with us, losing to what's younger, to what it used to be. But we say that it counts now.

Especially because we're connected by other people who have known each other for years, or who have met in person once or twice in Brooklyn. Maybe at Afropunk. Maybe we both know the partner of that person who used to host that queer night at that place that used to be something else.

Maybe I know someone who went to the same liberal arts school as them. Maybe they hosted a retreat in Bali in 2019, with someone I first met on Downelink. Maybe they haven't been able to do it since because of THE PANDEMIC, but also because they're back in school now. Maybe we share an ex of an ex. You might call that a same-ex relationship, and if you do, make sure you credit me and please buy my fucking book already, jeez.

But basically, we know each other by knowing or knowing of a lot of the same people or by looking like we'd know or know of a lot of the same people.

That's enough.

These days, we form a powerful group called a demographic. A group that buys and believes in similar ways and follows a lot of the same people / genres of people. A group that likes a lot of the same music and Spotify playlists. A group that is centering themselves and raising their plant children. A group that just monetized their hobby or their healing practice. A group that lives in a city that they love, that they moved to three to five years ago. A group that networks over tea and tarot, queering the language of money. A group that buys and buys into, yes. But buys and buys into as one, united. Unity moving units until we're (all) free, but some of us are more expensive.

I know that alternative money—money that you make as a result of healing yourself—spends differently, so I clap from afar at all their purchases and accomplishments. I like the photos. I comment on them.

I love this for y'all.

Anyway, the couple. We're close. I've followed them for seven years and they've been together for every last one. The one I interact with more has a thriving yoga practice, a thriving podcast, curates a lot of experiences, takes a lot of travel selfies, has a hard time saying no to training certifications. I like her captions because they're usually about unlearning the desire to conform to other people's expectations of who she/we should be. I feel proud to see her captions get to this place. To see her evolve into this new brand. The algorithm always allows me to see her, so I still know what she's up to. Obviously, that's comforting during these challenging times.

The one I interact with less is a professor, wears cool loc styles, likes to get dapper for an event, just started getting back into photography. Most of her photos are her getting back into photography. Sometimes there are captions about being Black. Sometimes there are stories from speaking events. The algorithm likes to surprise me with her, so I always have to manually go to her account, see where I start recognizing the shapes and colors of the grid. Always being behind on most of what's happening with her makes me feel less close to her. It's harder to root for her in the catch-up than it is in the just-now.

They got married two years ago, in Costa Rica, surrounded by people I recognized from social media and six whom I know from Atlanta. I clapped from afar with a like and a comment.

I love y'all for real.

We're so close that it's *almost* weird that I wasn't invited to the wedding, but I guess it's mostly not. The wedding looked pretty fun and *very* well done, and attending would have allowed me to meet all those people whom I follow, who follow me back. For the first time— all at once—at the wedding of a couple who didn't invite me, but who both thanked me for my comment in comments of their own, in the comment section of the one I interact with more.

A couple days later, I got the other one's wedding post. A set of black-and-white photos she'd taken, a caption that was a sweet dedication to her wife. I commented.

You're an amazing photographer! And congrats!

A few days later, she liked it. Said, *thanks, Jill.*

Over the past seven years, I'd dated many people, married, divorced, moved, fucked up, slain a dragon, been the dragon, laughed, taken too long, rushed through, made the wrong decision, got to the right place. Lived a life, seen it in real time, changed either all at once or not at all. And they—the wives—had seemingly changed

very little. Minorly. Only in fifteen seconds of a story. Only in a caption that was really just a sales pitch for a business that was really just
a caption.

I didn't mind. I was grateful for their selfless reliability. Their time-
line consistency stabilized my offline reality. I wasn't ever the same as
the last time I had been viewed, but from a distance, they were.

It's true that I couldn't offer to the people who followed me what
I wanted from the people I followed. I couldn't make myself show
up to social media, give a report on everything I was learning in the
real world, summarize all the biggest points, have my words resonate
hard enough with everybody to make me a big enough somebody.

But from them—the couple—I wanted as much as I could get and,
honestly, more.

When they wouldn't post each other for a while, I would panic.
I would worry that it was over and I'd never know the details, what
went wrong, who did what. Who would I decide to like more or less?
Who would I root for? Probably the wife I interacted with more, but
what if she was a liar? What if the whole time, I had been interacting
more with the wife who was to blame for their untimely end?

But then, on a Sunday in the summer, there they were. In the park,
with their dog and a blanket and Popsicles dripping in the sun, melt-
ing for the photo, leaning on each other with their eyes closed. Caption: *We're tired but we're still Black and we still love each other.*

It came from the one that I interact with less. Now that I'd had to
envision her being lied to, I felt closer to her. I was relieved that she
either hadn't been lied to or was into being lied to, so I commented.
Missed y'all. Glad to see you any time you pop up here.

She commented: *j i l l l l l* 🩶 🩶 🩶

It read as a hug. I could feel it wrap around me, comfort me with
its unearned familiarity.

And yet, I remembered a time when they would post each other
all the time. It wasn't this *We're still* _____ business. It's the word
"still" that worried me. Were they talking to us or each other?

A month later, the wife I interacted with less posted a selfie without the locs. The caption was: *New beginnings.*

I immediately texted my friend whom I'd met in real life, twice, years ago, and have communicated with online ever since. I asked her if she'd seen the haircut.

HER: Who's haircut?
　　Whose*
ME: The wives. The one who does the yoga. The professor with the locs. They live in LA. Somebody is a Gemini or they both are.
HER: yessssssssssss. I know them. They basically have the same chart and they talked about it on Live that one time and we were all like, ok but wow.
　　What happened?
ME: The professor cut her hair. She's talking about new beginnings.
HER: Noooooooooooooooooooooooooooooooooooooooo. We don't like new beginnings!
ME: Exactly! I was like, not a new beginnings haircut because the haircut is usually just the beginning of the new beginnings 😵
HER: They can't break up, tho.
ME: Why not? I mean, they can't I know. But why are you saying that?
HER: Didn't they just come on here talkin about how they're starting a couples advice YouTube or something? But like woke advice tho you know. Spiritual
ME: That wasn't them but I know who you're talking about and no. Stop.
HER: lol.
ME: I'm talking about the ones who got married in Costa Rica and everybody was there. It looked like the wedding planner was a human named black tumblr.
HER: not the wedding planner named black tumblr.
　　You're wild. ◆◆
HER: ohhhhh. I know who you mean. Whaaaaaaat?!
ME: That's what I'm saying!
HER: oh that shit is really over then because I saw the other one saying something about how you can't love someone

into healing themselves or something. you know. But
WOWWWWWW.

ME: fuck. They were all we had.

HER: they really were.

ME: I loved that wedding

HER: everybody did.

ME: Maybe they're fighting.

HER: I can't even picture them fighting like that for real

ME: I can't either, but they have to

HER: maybe they don't have to fight. Maybe some people don't
fight

ME: Wait. But you know that they fight.

HER: I bet they fight but different than the rest of us

ME: Probably.

HER: Yup they let the stars do the fighting.

ME: Stop it.

A few weeks later, they announced via matching posts that they could finally tell (us) what they'd been up to. There was a photo shoot in the redwoods, a baby bump visible through a cutaway, a series of embraces, a new beginning.

A few minutes later, I got a text that I knew was coming.

HER: Yooooooo. We were wrong.

ME: I know! I'm so happy we were!

HER: Me too!

Under each of their matching posts, I left a matching comment.
Congrats on new beginnings!
They each commented.
Thanks Jill!
The one I interacted with less commented almost immediately. Her wife commented the next day. Everything was back on track.

When the pregnant wife (whom I have more interaction with) was absent from social media, I didn't have to panic because of course she was! Why wouldn't she be? When she did show up, I was grateful.

Whether it was a "here y'all go" selfie, the camera angling down on her to show the thrown-togetherness of the outfit, the "I'm too pregnant to care" aesthetic, the captions reading like they'd been typed out with an eye roll and a shrug, or a photo of her meditating in the nursery that they'd just finished decorating, I was just glad to feel like everything was going well.

Until one afternoon, I heard the telltale text tone of a real-life friend.

HER: My friend who knows both of them says they're not together anymore
ME: Which both of them are you talking about?
HER: YOU KNOW WHO STOP PLAYING
ME: They're pregnant.
HER: THEY'RE DIVORCING
ME: Please with the caps.
HER: no cap they're divorcing
ME: Why would they divorce?
HER: Why did you?
ME: Too soon.
HER: Because they don't want to be together anymore I guess

I felt my body react to the news, the hope that the public could predict the personal leaving my body. If not them, then who? If not that, then what?

ME: They were supposed to make it.
HER: They were. But they were both Geminis, so we should have known
ME: Oh my God. That's right. We should've known.
HER: The stars know everything

That helped.

x x x x x x x

From: Alex ▮▮▮▮▮▮▮▮▮▮
To: Damon Young ▮▮▮▮▮▮▮▮▮▮
Subject: Racism Is Really Bad

A word.

In the fifth graf of "Racism Is Really Bad," you cite a story about a time your great-uncle applied for a home loan and wasn't able to receive it because, according to you, the bank didn't loan money to Black people. As you stated, the bank manager even personally came out of his office to tell him, "We don't loan money to your kind."

Your piece was definitely punctuated well and mostly legible, I'll give you that. But it falls apart when you center your premise around such a shaky story. Are you certain *"your kind"* was a reference to race? What evidence do you have to support that? The statistics? Where's the proof?

You later state that your great-uncle was a farmer, and that he enjoyed reading the newspaper while sitting on the porch. Tell me, since you're so smart, how do you know that the bank manager didn't just have an animosity for farmers or readers? Or perhaps even porches?

I know racism exists, I'm not denying that. But you do yourself no favors with these types of race-baiting hysterics.

Alex

x x x x x x x

You Gonna Get These Teeth

✴

DAMON YOUNG

Sometimes when I watch the Black male auteurs of the genre of performative fucking I wonder how much of what we do of what I do in the bedroom is derivative of what they did and I'm not talking about certain positions or even ass-slapping and choking or anything we might not have thought to want to do without witnessing a porn nigga do it first but language the articulation the specific cadence of instruction ("GIVE ME THAT PUSSY") and predictive expectation ("YOU GONNA GET THIS DICK") were niggas like Wesley Pipes just replicating how we had sex in real life then or were they virtuosos conjuring entire lexicons from imagination but anyway let's talk about teeth my teeth have always existed to me as both visual proof and a validating register of my self-consciousness this shit wasn't just in my head I've been called beaver and bucktooth and chipmunk and more because my teeth are big and because they developed gaps because my parents didn't have enough cash for braces so each time I opened my mouth it was a memoir a convergence of mortifications an orgy of shames wrestling for prime space in my brain so I found reasons to keep my mouth closed in pictures closed in conversation closed unnaturally when an open-mouth smile was expected there's a popular meme with Anthony Mackie where he's making the face he's known for making it's a face where his mouth looks closed by force a face like he's holding in a secret or a mouth-ful of Dr Pepper a face that a cat would make if they were capable of shame but when I see it I just see a man who is also known for hav-ing a gap between his two front teeth and probably developed that face from years of being teased about his teeth as a kid I know that face because that face was my face for years for decades for far too long but then I got some money from my book deal and from selling my blog it wasn't fuck-you money or even nigga-forget-you money but it was definitely excuse-me money and after I got my excuse-me money I bought an excuse-me car an excuse-me house some excuse-me sneakers and some excuse-me Invisalign in 2021 and even before they began to shift my teeth they immediately improved my grill because the trays you place in your mouth create an illusion of straight teeth when you open your mouth and so when I left the house for the first time with my new mouth I just had one thought in my head and that's YOU GONNA GET THESE TEETH I was a talking-ass smiling-ass motherfucker smiling at baristas smiling at squirrels smiling at my reflection in shallow puddles taking selfies for the first time with the camera all up in my face shameless smiles everywhere cause YOU GONNA GET THESE TEETH smiling to myself in the street when a thought about that time with that girl at that place during that time way back when just popped into my head I mean you know how these sorts of random microbursts of energy and cognizance and nostalgia are specifically engineered to induce a smile when they seep back into your consciousness regardless of where you happen to be but for me this type of experience was laced with the trauma of catching myself smiling by myself one time when I was on campus at Canisius and one of my teammates said that if he were me he'd never smile and I shot right back at him said you look like a six-foot sea-horse you bitch-ass nigga but shit like that happened enough to me for me to be smile-shy in public so YOU GONNA GET THESE TEETH to make up for all those pictures I'd take with friends and family and lovers where I'd be so happy but would look like I'd just experienced colonoscopy prep not the colonoscopy itself no those are fun as fuck a walk in the park a scoop of ice cream a welcome tickle but the prep makes you consume seventeen thousand liters of laxative over a seventeen-hour span and shit so much and so violently that you dry heave from your bootyhole not your anus no when it's exploding from you like a levee just broke in your booty the place it bursts out from is a bootyhole motherfucker so YOU GONNA GET THESE TEETH because I think I might actually be handsome now not a 10 or even an 8 but maybe a 6.8 or 7.2 which are dangerous earthquakes people might die I wouldn't dare call myself that before my new mouth I knew I wasn't the worst-looking man in the world and that is how I would have described myself on a dating profile if I ever had one but handsome was for different niggas for niggas with wide smiles who kept eye contact with you when they looked at you instead of being like me and not keeping eye contact for too long 'cause that would mean you were still looking at me and I'd want you to stop before you had enough time to really peep and critique and deconstruct my grill when my mom would say I was handsome I'd tell her thank you and then I'd think nigga why you lying but now if I had just one more phone call with her I'd ask her to stay undead for at least another hour because I'm coming up to see you and YOU GONNA GET THESE TEETH to finally validate your assessments but back to the eye contact thing it's funny and sad to think of all the traits and tics I developed from a lifetime commitment to opening my mouth as little as possible I take esomeprazole once a day for the acid reflux that's been fucking with me for twenty years it's under control now in a way it wasn't when it would cause so much pain that I couldn't lie down and sleep unless I stood under a scalding shower for an hour to let the water splash on my chest and maybe it's possible maybe maybe maybe maybe that the reflux maybe developed after years of eating too quickly not chewing to completion gulping instead of swallowing all things I learned to do to open my mouth as little as possible and maybe maybe maybe maybe actually definitely definitely definitely definitely definitely a lifetime of forced smirks and tight-lipped grimaces that existed instead of smiles formed lines in my face like how a couch cushion develops creases how rocks shift and erode after years of waves crashing into them how niggas who smile all the time have always smiled all the time look like they're always smiling so YOU GONNA GET THESE TEETH because I feel like I'm learning how to exist in the world again I think some of my smiles now are overcorrections on "No More Parties in LA" Kanye called himself the "thirty-eight-year-old eight-year-old" and that's how I feel now when I smile sometimes like for real there should be a class or something for niggas who just started smiling in public at forty to teach us when and when not to smile in conversation exactly how many seconds you can hold a woman's gaze before a smile is seen as a flirt how long you're allowed to smile while strolling down the street before niggas think you're a pedophile it's so strange now to be smiling back when people smile at me instead of racing through a cost-benefit analysis of whether it's safe to show them my teeth perhaps even my aversion to small talk is less about pretending to be interested in y'all's thoughts on cloud formations and alternative milks and more about just not trusting people enough to be vulnerable enough to keep my mouth open around them unless I absolutely had to I mean I'm not all of a sudden Mr. Small Talk now I don't need you to joke about how long the line is while we're both standing in it because I mean we're both standing in it so I already know but when it happens now instead of an anguished grin and a nod in your direction the bare minimum of socially acceptable response I'll say "Yes this line does seem to be long" with a smile as wide as my patience is for you and YOU GONNA GET THESE TEETH because I am taking better care of them now I mean I never neglected them I'd get checkups I'd brush twice a day I'd use mouthwash I'd floss on holidays but now the difference in care reminds me of the difference between how I'd treat my Dodge Charger and how I'd treat the Maserati I bought with my excuse-me money the Charger was taken care of sure washes oil changes and all the shit you do to maximize a car's use but the Maserati was getting detailed regularly and motherfucking massages and if you could give a car a blow job it would have got one of them too I hit a pothole once and got a flat and I didn't have a spare and there was a Pep Boys a block away so I drove to it and told one of the Pep Boys my predicament and he looked at me like "Nigga" and I looked at him like "What?" and he finally said "Nigga, this is Pep Boys. We don't work on Maseratis here" and while he didn't actually say "nigga" I could feel his inflection in my soul but yeah I don't have Pep Boys teeth anymore with Invisalign you have to wear the trays for twenty hours a day and can't eat or drink colorful or hot liquids with them in and each time you have to put the trays back in after eating you have to brush and floss first so I'm brushing and flossing like a madman like a motherfucker like a Maserati now my teeth are shiny these bitches are sparkly so YOU GONNA GET THESE TEETH I can't help but think though that since teeth in America have this inexorable relationship with class and since I allowed myself to feel deep shame for not having money and since I've had excuse-me money since 2016 maybe this new feeling is less about my new teeth and more of a new money learning curve where the shame slowly withered and made me more depleted of fucks about how you felt about my mouth I suspect it's a bit of both I give fewer fucks sure and my divestment of fucks is connected to my wallet and I think maybe the new teeth are a bank statement a long receipt a billboard of fucklessness stupid people say that money changes you smart people say that money changes how people treat you and whether you change or not is assessed through that lens and maybe maybe maybe maybe though that withering of shame is conspicuous contagious and niggas ain't responding different to me because of my mouth or my money but because the odor that shame emits is gone and a nigga smells sweet now so YOU GONNA GET THESE TEETH it's all a performance really which is the greatest lesson learned from Grand Chancellor Pipes and the rest of the artisans of the vernacular of fucking when you ask a woman "WHOSE PUSSY IS THIS?" the request itself exists in a shared state of accepted lunacy of course both practically and theoretically the pussy belongs to the person it's attached to you are merely visiting it it might as well be a time-share or the motherfucking Hirshhorn but the performance of sex sometimes involves the delusion of requesting that a woman loudly relinquish ownership of her body to you it's a question with no right answer except the wrong one and the irrational confidence necessary to ask it is something I always admired about those men a level of absurd tenacity I thought was aspirational I knew it was a show for the cameras and for the people watching at home and even for their partner(s) but it wasn't until I got older and started having sex and then got older and had more sex that I realized that the show was mainly for them mainly to squash any lingering doubts and self-consciousnesses to be so present in the moment that it transcends reality I mean delusion is necessary when dicks are so arbitrarily temperamental my smile isn't spotless now years of strange teeth have made them permanently imperfect even with three years of Invisalign but they are much straighter than they were before and I get sad sometimes now when I think about all the time I allowed shame to rob from me all of the years I convinced myself to shrink and I need to forgive myself for that so YOU GONNA GET THESE TEETH because I'm talking to myself now just like Chancellor Pipes did and YOU GONNA GET THESE TEETH because it's the best way to say I'm sorry.

The Karen Rights Act

MATEO ASKARIPOUR

T hey're ready for you, Ms. Knight," Karen said.

The older woman continued to stare out the Supreme Court building's second-floor window, the US Capitol building in her direct line of sight. "I'll be out in a second. But, Karen?"

"Yes, Ms. Knight?"

"Call me Karen."

"Yes . . ."

"*Karen.*"

"Yes, *K-K-Karen.*"

"It's not dirty, you know," the older woman said, finally turning around. "The K-word."

Her new assistant, dressed in white pants, a white blouse, and a white cardigan, hugged her notebook tighter, her eyes touching everything in the room except her boss's face. "I know. I've read your book. Been to the meetings. But—"

"Self-hate is very real. You have to chip away at it, bit by bit, day by day. But before you know it, you'll only be left with the beautiful core of who you are, and no one will be able to take that away from you."

The young woman's eyes and mouth softened. "Thank you, Karen. I'll see you in the courtroom." She left as quietly as she'd come, the heavy wooden door giving a tiny *click* as it closed.

Karen Lanie Knight—KLK as the world, yes, the *world,* referred to her with equal parts admiration and derision—went back to the window overlooking the oval plaza and thought about how the neoclassical building she stood in was a testament to justice, when justice was the very thing deprived of her and her sistren. Until today, the day when everything would change, when all she'd sacrificed and fought for would finally come to sweet fruition. Bittersweet, that is.

Because there is nothing delicious about having your one-year-old boy, blond hair and blue eyes, the picture of perfection, taken from you. There is nothing mouthwatering about losing your job, a job you'd dedicated a decade and a half of your life to despite the advances that the "Your hands make me hard"–texting CEO made toward you; the havoc that the organization you worked for wreaked on innocent people; the media storm that you were forced to weather "for the good of the company." There is nothing appetizing about being crucified over five letters that were thrust upon you, like a blanket of smallpox, leading to your eventual demise and the destruction of those who were your kin—not by choice but by fate. Fighting to justify your humanity is shit, regardless of how hard people work to sugarcoat it.

The thing is, no one knows the true origin of *Karen.* Some claim it has been with us since before humanity as we know it—middle-aged white Neanderthal women, clubs in hands, threatening to alert the loinclothed authorities if they didn't get the *exact* piece of bison they wanted. Others associate it with more recent events: a Black bird-watcher having the cops called on him; white women assuming the role of police by prohibiting Black people from parking in certain places, hosting barbecues, working out in the gym—just living too loudly for their liking, really.

But the origin never mattered to KLK, only the outcome. At first, she and her husband laughed at the memes—white women with long, side-swept bangs, more layers than the Earth's crust, and spiky, shorter hair in the back, with "Let me speak to your manager!" written in large white text across the top and bottom of the images. She laughed when the internet canceled Karens in Walmarts across the country. She laughed until only two years ago, when she tried walking into a Brother Jimmy's BBQ in midtown Manhattan and the bouncer asked for her ID.

"ID? You sure know how to flatter a woman. Do I look younger than thirty-nine?"

The bouncer, used to patrons fishing for compliments, smirked and held out his baseball mitt of a hand until she deposited her license. After a quick scan, he said, "No can do."

"No can do?" She looked to her friend Janice and laughed. "It clearly says I'm thirty-nine."

"And," he said, bending his redwood-tree frame toward her, "it also clearly says your name is Karen. Can't you read?" He pointed to a sign in the bar's window that read, NO KARENS, NO DOGS, NO INCELS.

She stood there a moment longer, waiting for him to crack, for him to open his arms and say, "You've been punked!," but he only stood there, waving a slew of people in before he looked at Janice and said, "Coming or going?"

"Let's just go somewhere else," Janice said, tugging Karen from the bar. But when they went to others, from the quietly wealthy Upper East Side to the loudly rich Financial District, they were met with the same refusals. Each bar had a sign in its window that was a variation on the first: NO KARENS, NO CATS, NO JORDAN PETERSON. NO KARENS, NO RABBITS, NO BITCOIN BROS. NO KARENS, NO HEDGEHOGS, NO HIPSTERS.

Tired of the abuse, she went home and told her husband, Connor, what had happened. "It's probably just some collective prank," he said, bouncing Hewlett, their one-year-old, on his knee as he tried to feed him some applesauce.

"Yeah," Karen said, shaken. "Probably something to do with Tik-Tok."

The next day, her boss, Aiden, called her into his office. "I'm sorry to tell you, Karen, but today's your last day."

"You're kidding."

"Unfortunately, I'm not."

"For what? I'm the top salesperson here. Not saleswoman, not salesman, *salesperson*! Do you know how many lower-incomed people I've pressured into buying our shitty life insurance?"

He leaned back and threw his hands up. This bastard had been cleaning toilets when Karen found him, and he'd not only leapfrogged his way into being her boss, but now *he* was firing *her*. "I know, I know. None of it is fair. But we received a new mandate from the powers that be, and all Karens are out. You—I mean they—are bad for our image."

She looked through the glass window in Aiden's office. A middle-aged Black woman, also named Karen, was doing some kind of dance at the photocopier. "That means Karen Whitestone too, right?"

"No. According to the memo, only white women named Karen are part of the . . . redundancies. Karen Whitestone loves Martha Stewart and hockey, it's true, but she wasn't on the list."

"I'm dreaming," she said to herself as she walked out of the building, arms struggling to carry the storage box containing, among other items, her neon pink Nalgene, her worn Moleskine, a few bags of SkinnyPop popcorn, and her old Johnson & Wales hoodie. Her Tory Burch flats chauffeured her from the Flatiron office where she'd previously worked into Madison Square Park, and without even realizing it, she was calling Connor, but it went straight to voicemail. She called the daycare where they sent Hewlett, and when the receptionist answered, she said that Connor had picked up Hewlett and left. *That's strange.*

She called Connor again, but it went straight to voicemail. And again. And again. And again. A hot anvil dropped from her heart to the floor of her stomach. She had to go home, but the subway wouldn't get her to the West Village fast enough, so she went to order an Uber, but when she opened the app, it said, ACCESS DENIED. The same with Lyft. The same with Gett. The same with Via. The same with the few woman-focused rideshare apps she'd downloaded in solidarity but never actually used. ACCESS DENIED. ACCESS DENIED. ACCESS DENIED. It was only when she stuck her hand out for a cab and one passed a Black couple who had been waiting longer to immediately serve her that she breathed easier. Some things hadn't changed.

"Hello," she said, dropping the box onto the back seat and scooting inside. "Bleecker and Charles Street, please."

"Sure thing," the man, who could've been Greek or some other brand of off-white European, replied. "Got ID?"

Not this again. "No," she said, realizing she was using a voice she didn't know was inside of her; some might've called it her *Let me talk to your manager* voice. "Just drive." The man did as he was told.

She raced out of the taxi and up the stairs of her town house, thrust her key into the lock, and turned, but it stopped. She pulled it out, confirmed it was indeed her house key, and tried again, but it didn't budge. Her neighbor on the floor above her, Kenan, stuck his head out his window and said, "Connor and Hewlett left a few hours ago. And Bryan told me that you're evicted because, and I quote, 'This shit isn't worth it.'"

"What?" The world was spinning around her. Maybe there was something in the smoothie she'd had that morning, the chickpea salad from last night. This, none of this could be real.

Kenan pulled his head inside, then she heard, "But good news! Connor left this," and out flew her lavender, medium-size Rimowa suitcase—a gift from Connor for her last birthday. It landed at the bottom of the stairs with a thud.

Her neighbor was closing his window when she said, "Kenan," and he paused. "I don't know what's happening, but everyone—no, every white woman named Karen—is being persecuted, like some sort of twenty-first-century witch hunt. Please, I'm begging you, let me inside your apartment so I can figure out what to do next."

Her plea was met with silence; then he jutted his head out the window, stared down at her, and rained spit as he cackled. "What, you think I don't remember you sending Bryan an email after my last party? He forwarded it to me. You said . . . what was it? 'Please ensure that Kenan keeps his *ghetto* activities to a minimum. This is the West Village, after all.'"

"I—" The window slammed shut.

No one, including her parents in Boston, would take her in. Over-night, the world had become a dangerous place for Karens and anyone who dared to harbor them. She found herself horizontal on a bench in Washington Square Park—bank account frozen, cell phone service cut, Connor and Hewlett nowhere to be found—sleeping until Ignorant Karen Enforcement (IKE) picked her up, tossed her in the back of a van with blue-, green-, and hazel-eyed white women staring back at her with a feral quality, their J.Crew T-shirts, Lululemon leggings, and Madewell jeans ripped and dirtied.

"Please," one woman screamed through the grate of the van's steel partition, "I'd like my phone call."

The two IKE agents, a Black man and a Black woman, looked at each other, then laughed so hard that the man doubled over, slapping the dashboard, and the woman, driving, almost hit a yellow hydrant.

Karen didn't know how long she'd been in the van when they arrived at a nondescript building—bright spotlights cutting through the dark summer night—that could have been a Target as easily as it could have been a Nordstrom. The IKE agents marched them inside and down a path bordered by chain-link fences with middle-aged white women huddled behind them. A few of them crooned "Hello" by Adele, the desperation heavy in their voices. Some, Karen could tell by the rhythmic clapping, played patty-cake. And others were repeating ingredients for what she realized were their homemade variations on mac and cheese: "Box of Kraft with cauliflower, vegan cheddar, and bologna mixed in. The kids will love it."

The next year was hell.

Bare lettuce with mayonnaise as a dipping sauce. Agents forcing them to reenact scenes from *Mean Girls* (2004), *10 Things I Hate About You* (1999), and even *Hamilton* (2015). Makeshift paint-and-sips with ninety-nine-cent Pinot Grigios that had been left to oxidize, resulting in every woman vomiting on herself and the others.

Karen patiently bided her time and did what the agents ordered. She slowly befriended one of them, bonding with her over their love of Michelle Obama, and it was this agent who smuggled her a burner phone with 14 percent battery. Karen then made a call to a college friend, Cayleigh, who had become a lawyer at the ACLU. Her middle name was Karen—thus saving her from a similar fate but sparking the ever-powerful brand of "Am *I* next?" fear in her—and she promised to work on their cause.

As Cayleigh got to work, Karen began to organize the women in the middle of the night, whispering about their disenfranchisement, urging them to hold fast to secure their freedom, and forming what would later be known as Karen's Keepers (KKs), the first and largest advocacy group for Karen rights. The IKE agent, whom Karen would never disclose the identity of, lest she be terrorized for being a Karen lover, would charge the burner phone and return it to Karen while her sistren distracted the other agents. This allowed her to send tear-filled emails to abolitionist lawmakers, social media influencers, and their staunchest supporters, former Avon ladies.

Three months later, Cayleigh—pantsuit, thigh gap, and all— appeared at the IKE center, smiling next to a sullen agent. "You're out," the man said.

Cayleigh explained that a certain celebrity-turned-politician owed her a favor, leading to Karen's special dispensation. Before leaving, Karen hugged her weeping sisters, promising to return, like Moses, and free them all.

Thus began the Karen Rights Era. Karen, now widely known as KLK, along with Cayleigh, wasted no time in getting her story out. Given that every outlet from CNN to Fox wanted to boost their ratings, they brought her on, subjecting her to ridicule and gaslighting, but she wouldn't be deterred. Armed with only courage and a desire for a better tomorrow, she shared her story, the story of 1.4 million Karens living in the United States. She was invited to debate eugenicists at every Ivy League and respected institution of higher learning, including an esteemed professor from MIT who demanded that her brain waves and cranium be studied. Death threats flooded her inbox, and when people found out where she was living—a Dumbo penthouse rented in Cayleigh's name, paid for by anonymous donors— they stood outside, 24/7, waving signs that read CRY, KAREN, CRY!, I AM YOUR MANAGER, BITCH!, and even GRAB THEM BY THE BOB!

"Don't worry," Cayleigh said one day, hand on KLK's shoulder as they looked down at that day's mob. "Darkness cannot drive out darkness; only light can do that. Hate cannot drive out hate; only love can do that."

"Jesus, that's good. Who said that?"

"You know, I'm not sure. Jesse Jackson. Nelson Mandela. Snoop Dogg. One of them."

"Whoever it is was right."

It was those words that prompted her to write *The K Word:* a memoir and call to arms for all who wanted to vanquish the dark with the light. She'd written it in a frenzy, subsisting only on kale chips and Evian, and she finished it in a month. Cayleigh now tripled as her friend, lawyer, and book agent, and though almost no publisher wanted to touch the Karen Lives Matter movement with a ten-foot polo stick, an imprint of Simon & Schuster, Balanced Books, believed in her, giving her a modest $500,000 advance.

The book would become an instant number one *New York Times* bestseller. And with that momentum Cayleigh and KLK sued every single bar that had discriminated against her; her former employer; her old landlord, Bryan; and even her ex-husband, Connor. Hollywood execs soon came knocking, begging her for the chance to executive produce a series based on her time in the IKE center, tentatively titled *Karen Is the New Black.*

From having seen how the media, and world, focused on the plight of Black people in 2020—DEI initiatives, Black squares on social media, and denouncements appearing faster than you can say "Beetlejuice, Beetlejuice, Beetlejuice!"—only for them to forget about it once progress was no longer in vogue, she knew she had to do whatever she could do, *now,* to fight for her rights—peeling them, one by one, from the brittle claws of nameism. The Supreme Court, wanting to get this over and done with before someone burned down Beverly Hills, agreed to hear the case directly, instead of forcing KLK, Cayleigh, and the hundreds of thousands of others who comprised their class-action lawsuit to go through lower appeals courts, which is how we arrive at this present moment: an American hero staring out the window of the Supreme Court building, awaiting her fate and the fate of over a million other women.

Cayleigh and her team had argued magnificently. Character witnesses were paraded around like models dressed in homeless chic at a Balenciaga show. One woman even brought her two-month-old baby girl, named Karen in protest, who looked like nothing more than a sack of spoiled dough. She held her up for all the court to see and asked a question that was immediately turned into a headline: "WHAT DID *SHE* DO?" If there was anything to turn public sentiment, it was that. KLK slapped her forehead, cursing herself for not bringing out a white baby named Karen sooner, quickly penning a new motto to be included in future printings of *The K Word:* "If you want a problem solved, get a white baby involved."

And solved it was. When KLK thrust open the court chamber's oak doors, heels clacking on the bloodred marble as she passed between two Ionic columns, the air was still. Clarence Thomas, delivering the opinion of the majority, cried as he gave an impassioned reading of the summary, stating, "A world without Karens is a world I don't want to live in." The decision was eight to one in favor of federally prohibiting discrimination "on the basis of name." The world was spinning around Karen for the second time in her life, but instead of moving against her, it was with her.

She didn't drink any champagne or attend any parties. She didn't linger on the courthouse steps, basking in the freedom she had won for women who, like her, were treated unfairly for no reason other than that this mad world could. Instead, she went home, and Connor, finding a sliver of a conscience that wasn't court-ordered, brought three-year-old Hewlett over, finally giving Karen the chance to hold her son again.

The next day, her assistant, Karen, arrived. In her hands was a stack of mail. "You go put some coffee on," KLK said, "and I'll sort through this junk, okay?"

"It's a plan," the young woman replied, beaming.

Fan mail. Bills. Fan mail. Bills. A letter from the New York City Civil Court. She tore open the envelope, and inside was a response to a name-change petition she'd filed almost two years ago, on a whim, after those bouncers turned her away from their bars. Back then, it was just a manifestation of her frustration, not a serious attempt to go from Karen Lanie Knight to something more socially acceptable. But there it was, in plain black letters:

Dear Ms. Johnson,

It's my pleasure to inform you that your name-change petition, KAREN LANIE KNIGHT to LASHONDA JOHNSON, has been approved.

Please accept our sincerest apologies for the process having taken this long. As I'm sure you can imagine, we were backed up with tens of thousands of petitions, and are continuing to work through them steadily, with unwavering focus.

The name change is effective immediately. The IRS, DMV, and SSA have all been notified, but it is your responsibility to update your records, and obtain both a new driver's license and a social security card by reaching out to those respective organizations.

Thank you,
Brenda Smith
New York City Civil Court

The letter fell from Lashonda's hands, fluttering to the hardwood like an injured butterfly. Her assistant entered the living room, holding two steaming mugs from Anthropologie with "K" monogrammed on each of them.

"Karen," the young woman said through a confused smirk, "everything okay? You look like you just saw a ghost."

Unmurdered in Grandma's Kitchen

✳

ALEXANDER HARDY

My grandma don't like niggas in her kitchen.

"I don't like people hovering over my shoulder when I'm working," she would declare. "I'm not putting on a show."

This was her diplomatic way of letting us know that, when she was making magic happen, whether she was in Two-Oven Mode or not, the kitchen, her art studio, was not a destination for breathing, loitering, or socializing.

Since her arrival with her husband and children in Hampton, Virginia, from Panama City, Panama, in 1970, Miss Ruby has cultivated a reputation for providing fellowship and connections for housing, employment, and business; hosting and catering parties; and sharing abundant meals made with love and familiar, soul-filling flavors with other children of the Plantain Belt adjusting to life in an unfamiliar city with colorless homes and not enough gold teeth per capita.

Her kitchen sits in the middle of her home, connecting the den/ party room and plant-filled Florida room to the rest of the house, but you better not even consider dreaming about the possibility of thinking about casting thine peasant eyes on her bountiful stove or any of its glorious fruits without power-washing your hands. Twice, perhaps.

On the wall opposite the kitchen's entrance, alongside a row of pictures and paintings of family members, there is a clock commemorating Grandpa Johnny's time with the Hampton, Virginia, sheriff's department (1978 to 1991), a photo of Aunt Rita the Model striking a pose on a beach at sunset in a green cutout bathing suit, and various cursive prayers. There's a plaque that Johnny (and the US Air Force) presented to her "for her perseverance and devotion to duty in maintaining home and family" while he was over yonder in Vietnam shortly after they arrived in the country.

These sit across from the photo of Uniformed Johnny and the Dapper Conked Man with the Pipe and the grayscale painting of a seated Conked Johnny with his arms around one knee. My cousins and I used to joke that the smirk on Conked Johnny was because he knew you probably hadn't washed your hands good enough.

Only the trusted and preapproved, vetted through decades of Panamanian-flavored friendship or prior experiences in the culinary trenches, get the right to engage in stovetop sorcery here. She rarely eats other people's cooking, so if she grants you the right to hold cooking utensils, heat and manipulate food, and combine ingredients for consumption in her kingdom, a privilege revocable if she decides she "can just do it real quick, but you can still watch," she trusts you and believes your food won't shame her legacy or maim the guests.

And you get twelve years added on to your life.

Striving to earn her trust and respect as a cook and baker is a recurring theme in my character's multiseason arc, so I occasionally stress to impress her with my kitchening feats.

And she be like, "That sounds interesting," or "Oh, no, you don't have to bring any. I have plenty of food here. Thank you."

The day after my oldest niece, Tianna, graduated from high school, we hosted a pancake brunch for her friends and the family at my grandma's house.

My niece wanted to keep it simple. This means Grandma didn't need to roll out the buffet setup, the light shows, and the Full Miss Ruby Experience. We told her she didn't need to spend days cooking or retrieve the Olympic-size rice cauldrons from storage.

"We're keeping it simple," we told her.

We wanted her to enjoy herself as well. My sister brought the food: bacon, eggs, juice, fruit, and a box of pancake mix. Someone brought a cake. Grandma handled the cooking and warmed some empanadas.

She cooked the bacon and added salt, garlic, and pepper to the eggs before scrambling them. My sister opened the box of pancake mix and cut open the corner of the plastic bag inside. Grandma, who makes salad dressing, hot sauce, short sets, and bread from scratch, stared at the box for a while.

"What you mean, just add water?" she said, twisting up her face with disbelief. "How that make a pancake?"

"It has everything in the mix already, Mom. They did the work for you. You can add whatever you like to the batter. You can use milk, add spices, whatever you want."

Grandma examined the box. She was disgusted. "And you eat that?"

"Yes, Mom."

My sister and I agreed. Grandma opened the cabinet above the second oven.

"I can just put something together real quick . . ." She unrolled and looked inside a near-empty bag of flour and sucked her teeth. She'd had just enough to complete a large empanada order a few days prior.

She wanted to go to the grocery store.

"Mom. The kids are hungry," my mom said. "You should just let Alex make the pancakes."

Thunder clapped.

I clenched my jaw while my stomach did a cute ribbon dance, but nobody burst into flames.

"It's okay. He can cook."

"Hmm." Grandma turned to look me up and down as if inspecting a used deep freezer at a garage sale. "You seen him cook?" she said as she considered multigenerational transfer-of-power terms.

"Yup."

Grandma and I had been making plans for me to gain access to the Empanada Arts the next time she had a big order. Because her memory was starting to falter a bit more, I wasn't sure if she remembered that she had agreed to consider my application. She hadn't seen me cook, though, so until I gained enough points to cross the bridge into the Land of Grandmotherly Approval, I was but another person hungry for the recipe for the phattest patties on the block.

I didn't even have any gold teeth.

I tried to convey my earnestness, deference, and intention to complete the task at hand without burning her castle down through telepathy, but my transmitter must've been off.

Until then, I had only been licensed to wash dishes (with supervision).

I held my breath and pumped two squirts of hand soap into my palm. As the water warmed up, I lathered soap up my forearms and tried to scrub all my sins away like I was preparing for surgery.

"The griddle is down there." Exhale.

Oh, snap. Now I had to prepare food and not kill everyone in front of her.

When I first took hold of the whisk after emptying the pancake mix into the bowl, I felt like I was about to rap for a record deal. But did I remember how to mix pancake batter? Was I holding the whisk right?

Did I remember how to flip pancakes?

Miss Ruby's ban on unvetted kitchen access prevents culinary horrors at the hands of lesser beings and also keeps spies and offspring alike from observing, learning, replicating, or passing down her spells.

There is no worn scroll detailing the ingredients, processes, or tricks.

Grandma isn't of the "Gather 'round, children, join me on bended knee and let me teach you the Way" variety when it comes to her legendary recipes and family favorites. Any offspring knowledge of the wizardry behind her fried rice with chicken, steak, and shrimp, her hot pepper sauce (which she sold by the case and shipped nationwide for a while), her stew chicken, her fried bakes, came through decades of immersion and reverse engineering their own approximation through tricky trial and humbling error.

"I do cooking, not cooking lessons," is how she refused to teach me her fried rice.

Even as my grandmother's second-oldest child and only daughter, my mother taught herself to cook after moving into her first apartment with my father, cultivating her own interpretation of our family's food-based love language. She, too, became a brilliant and generous self-taught cook.

My uncle is *still* trying to nail her mustard-based hot pepper sauce's sweet heat.

Grandma once told me that when it came to entertaining, she was "a one-woman show," striking a pose with her hands on her hips. She didn't outsource empanada crimping or benefit from an extra set of hands handling rice duties while cooking for crowds of gold-toothed revelers in her home or a dining hall.

That's why this box of pancakes was so important. First: buttery breakfast cakes in front of all these witnesses who would survive to tell the tale. Then washing dishes without supervision. Finally, after judging by the Elder Council based on the strength of my handwashing, my personal cleanliness, a skills assessment, and whether her feet were hurting: empanada apprenticeship.

My family gathered around like fight spectators.

I planted my feet on the emerald tiles beside the stove and reached into her cabinet, past the spice blends in containers labeled MEAT, PORK, CHICKEN, and RUBY MIX, to find her catering-size containers of cinnamon and nutmeg. I sprinkled until the ancestors said, "All right, now." I found vanilla extract next to a giant red-and-white metal tin of Sexton mace seasoning that might have been a relic of pre–Janet Jackson America. I splashed and whisked. Grandma hovered. Mom smiled.

"Don't overwhip the batter."

"Okay."

I melted butter in the skillet to call forth the crispy edges and remembered to breathe.

After inspecting my first round of pancakes, she left and went into her bedroom. I'd passed.

My uncle Andre walked into the kitchen as I flipped a pancake onto the stack and asked, "She know you cooking on her stove? How you get to cook here?"

I didn't need to say, "Because I'm a bad bitch," because he knew.

The warmth of activating favorite-grandchild superpowers surged throughout my body.

Everyone made it home unmurdered.

For weeks after the brunch, when I saw her or talked to her by phone, she reminded me of the endurance required to take this empanada journey with her. She warned me again one time when dropping off a container of fried rice.

"You might have to spend two days with me if you want to learn the patties."

"That sounds like a good time to me."

"Because I don't buy my empanada discs, you know."

"Of course not."

"I make my dough by hand, you know."

"I know."

"I don't get it from the store like some people."

I considered the countless good and terrible empanadas housed in stranger-made discs I'd demolished on the streets of Nueva York.

"It's not just some quick thing, you know."

"You take your time with each one."

"I make my meat one day. And I let it rest, you know. And then I rest. And then I make my dough the second day, so it's fresh. And I put them together," she said, crimping an imaginary patty in her hand.

"And that's why I tell you to charge more for them."

She reminded me that she never measures, so I'd have to watch closely.

"Hopefully, it don't slow me down too much," she said, and sighed. She looked worried.

"I'm a fast learner." Please validate me.

"Well . . ." She bent to hug my mom before leaving. "We'll see about that."

She finally showed me the Miss Ruby Method while preparing an order for eight dozen patties. She was making ten dozen—"Because I keep some for me and to give to people," she said.

I didn't tell her that some of us were worried about losing the wealth of culinary knowledge she held. That we strategized about absorbing and amplifying her wisdom and ways as she cooked and catered less and skipped or misused ingredients in dishes she'd made hundreds or thousands of times due to her dance with dementia.

I just thanked her each time she reminded me that using measuring cups and measuring spoons to bring her crescent-shaped gems together was slowing her down.

When she reminded me that she doesn't use written recipes, I told her, "That's why you need to show somebody how you make your food. So we don't lose those dishes."

She didn't miss a beat: "I'm not going anywhere." And that was the end of that.

She helped me manage my anxiety about crimping my way toward perfection and making patties in the same universe and bloodline as her.

"Well, first of all you have about sixty more years of practice ahead of you. Don't get too worked up about it. My ugly patties taste just as good."

I told her that made me feel good, to know she still made ugly patties.

"Y'all don't see those because I just eat the ugly ones myself. I been doing this awhile so I eat a lot of patty over the years. I have a reputation to protect, you know."

Who Cries in Waffle House?

ASHON CRAWLEY

John

And this is how I remember it. I said to him, *I want to be able to look at you and not be so hurt by you.* I can't remember if I said it in person but I'm quite shy so it's likely I said it while we were on the phone. I really wanted to date him. He was short and cute, though he had a big head. A student at Morehouse but home for the summer in Philly, I at the University of Pennsylvania. He was animated and fun to be with mostly. It was my first time really attempting something explicitly. Though I was confused about how it would all work. Because of my commitments to god, to church, to directing choirs and being a musician.

I enjoyed his company. Or at least the recollection of him some twenty-five or so years later makes me feel like I enjoyed a lot of his presence. He came to my apartment the first time I made turkey spaghetti. It was too spicy but I made it spicy because I wanted to mask the taste of ground turkey. It was my first time using it, a not-first-but-certainly-ongoing attempt to be healthy. We weren't on keto and low-carb things back then.

He visited what was my first apartment at Fortieth and Chestnut, on the third floor of the building with the Hair Hut salon owned by the white dude who was quite terrible on the bottom floor. I never met my second-floor neighbor the entire time I lived there, a bit over a year. My first terrible couch with springs that stuck out of the upholstery. My terrible full-size bed that I loved because it was the first time I'd slept on something larger than a twin. I felt grown. My thirteen-inch television that I borrowed from a friend because I could not afford my own. So many firsts in that apartment.

I determined that cooking would be a way I'd show my affection, a way for me to practice care, to show that I desired. And the hope was for the food to be a sensual thing shared, so much so that he would desire me.

He came over and we ate my turkey spaghetti and watched a movie. I don't remember which one. This was before the advent of Netflix, and thus the chill that came along with the DVDs-then-streaming platform. We watched whatever we watched but there was absolutely no *chill* to speak of. He left as quick as he came over, we likely didn't do more than shake hands the entire time, didn't sit directly next to each other—a feat because the couch was so very tiny.

I began watching romantic comedies when I was a kid. I loved, and still do love, so many of them. And if you know me you know I will talk excitedly about *Runaway Bride*—when she gives the dude the shoes is when I tear up and it doesn't matter that I have nothing in common with her. The idea of love always fascinated me.

I want to be able to look at you and not be so hurt by you, I said. A line from *The Object of My Affection* that Jennifer Aniston's character cries to the white gay boy she fell in love with. They flirted, and for a moment love that would be erotic and sexual was possible. That line remained with me, moved me. Even if it's hokey and embarrassing. I didn't cry when I said it to him but I certainly meant it—looking at the pic he sent through the AOL platform, or perhaps ICQ or College Club or the Black gay men chat room on Go.com, would give me butterflies, mostly because I wondered if he'd be my first real live boyfriend. Even if we'd only hung out twice.

The anticipation of his reply did not prepare me.

Then don't look at my picture, he said.

It stung. But who, seriously, quotes a romantic comedy, especially when the thing said didn't bring the two people together? You just have to laugh.

Anthony

Years later, a week or two before leaving Philly for good, I met up with another cute dude I initially met on Adam4Adam.com. I can still remember his profile picture—a wide-striped shirt and maybe jeans. We met in 2005 so the pics we could upload were still janky; his was ashy. It was a great time, even if we both were drunkenly flirty. We'd gone to Copabanana in Center City, had too many margaritas, made out on Spruce Street on the side steps of the Kimmel Center. I left the same year but he and I remained loosely in touch. So when I was visiting again maybe three or four years later, we decided to go out again. I wanted to see him again, hopefully rekindle and maybe move further into something. What I remember from that second, three-or-four-years-later visit is that we went to see some movie and he refused to sit next to me in the theater, which was nearly empty, and instead sat one row in front and one seat to the right of me. He said it was because he wasn't out and he didn't want people to think that we were on a date because also, I found out while we were on a date, *we were not on a date.* It was bad. I was offended. This wasn't the same fun, flirty thing from a couple years ago—this wasn't fun at all. But I still had to laugh.

We were both members of a message board on *#thatsite*. If you know, you know, as the kids say. So imagine my surprise when some-one posted a question about terrible dates, and I read about ours from his perspective. The way he described our interaction made me laugh. Loudly. Because the absurdity of the situation was also something awkward and silly and unfortunate. Sometimes you don't click. Sometimes you don't enjoy the presence of another. But I also began learning that there are different stages of queer life—that even if you're out, there is no guarantee that you will be in the same place in terms of comfort or have the same ideas about desire or under-stand sexuality in similar ways.

Terry

He asked if I came every night, he asked why I showed up nightly to Steamworks around two thirty in the morning. I was in Seattle for a summer job and had a lot of free time. So I would go to the Pig'N Whistle bar in my neighborhood nightly—so much so that they gave me a going-away party when I left, complete with a pig stuffed animal. The bartender-turned-friend heard me talk about my love for stuffed animals so she gifted me one. I'd drink my vodka sodas while reading or writing my dissertation. And I'd catch a cab afterward.

My first time in a sex club was in 2009, in Halifax, Nova Scotia. A friend told me about his time in one and I was curious. I was drunk. It was mostly empty. But the towel they gave me upon entry was warm. And it was a respectful experience, one with a lot of consent. You could refuse and they wouldn't get angry. You could pursue and have a momentary fling. I did both. I knew I would visit again.

In Seattle I went nightly because I was seeking connection. I imagined seeing someone in the steam, and smiling, and leaving together—finding love in a hopeless place. But who looks for a relationship in bathhouses? I went nightly because I grew up in the intense world of Black Pentecostalism. What we believed about god had to be experienced deep in the flesh, and we had to commit to it as a way of life. Church was episodic but the spiritual practice was a daily process. So though I left church, I always sought intensity.

And it wasn't until he asked me why I visited nightly that I even thought he noticed. Embarrassed because I didn't know how to say I'm lonely and I need love. I was almost always there with a handful of others so love would not find me there.

At Steamworks, on the back side steps of the Kimmel Center on Spruce Street kissing a boy in Philly, and repeating lines from terrible movies, I was seeking the kind of connection that I'd always desired, the kind that I saw on romantic comedies, that gave me a kind of unrequited hope.

Terrence

I have all kinds of stories about restaurants.

There was the Spaghetti Warehouse—and it had to be bad because the name was awful. He and I argued about something, left the restaurant early, and on the ride home, I got out of the car and walked to my destination. I don't remember his name or even the nature of the disagreement. But it was bad enough to leave.

There was, likely in 2017 right before I left, some dude I met on Grindr. It was a lukewarm restaurant with lukewarm water, which would have been fine had I not ordered the spicy tonkotsu. As dude and I talked and I ate, a trickle of sweat rolled down the back of my ear. Then another stream of sweat. I took the napkin and wiped. Then my forehead. I wiped more. Then my entire body exploded in heat. I asked the server for more water—cold—and they brought out more iceless lukewarm water that made me angry because it was right on the edge of cool. And the glasses were child size. Eventually I just asked for the pitcher. I gulped it down as I began to sweat through my shirt and hat. I never saw him again but I didn't care. I laughed the entire drive home.

It's funny, really. *Not ha-ha funny.* But have you ever cried in a Waffle House?

It happened again right before the onset of the pandemic in 2020. We'd been spending time together, too much time. Hours in my house. Text messages. Phone calls. That time he came over and left after seven and a half hours, at one forty-five a.m. There was the hug before he left and it was a moment's pause too long. There were butterflies shared. There was joy and laughter. The serious questions, the furrowed brows. The jokes, the easiness of breath and breathing when with each other.

And there was the soon-coming day. That one Sunday. The *It's a beautiful day you should leave the house* he said and the *Well pick me up* I said and him arriving and turning off the car and getting out of the vehicle and ringing the doorbell and smiling when I opened the door. The walk through the comic book store. The shared cupcake. The walk to that one place. The walk to that other place. The opening of the door and his hand placed on my lower back. This cannot *not* be a thing. Jennifer Aniston had nothing on me, on us.

It was the gesture. It was unspoken because it was reflexive and though neither one of us expected it, it happened.

And we continued. And there was talk about love. And talk, too, about disappointment. And neither one of you wanted dinner to end. And you asked about children. And he hedged. And you said *We should go on a real date* and he disappeared for a week. And you had breakfast at Waffle House a week later. And you asked what he was doing the rest of the day. And he told you he was taking that woman from some city some two hours or more away to a casino, that he didn't even know if she liked casinos, but he'd been stressed and needed to get away. And right there, in Waffle House, you cried. And you would have said, if you could have said, *I want to be able to look at you and not be so hurt by you.*

But tears were the only bravery you could muster. Because there was nothing to prepare you. You were not expecting it. There was no movie or song or novel plot that felt the way you felt.

Because his was both not a response to the question of the date, and a refusal to respond to what the question of the date was really saying, asking—what are we doing? do you feel it too? do you feel what I feel? who am I to you? who are we to each other? We already care, let's continue. But the answer was also a buffer to saying the very explicit *no* I was supposed to but did not, could not, understand. After the intimacy shared that was real, that not even friends could deny, the very small unanswered question left me exhausted, moved me to tears.

Jerrod

Some knew the title before watching and, so, likely knew what the secret reveal of his name would be before they watched. I'd seen tweets about *Rothaniel* but I'd never seen the sitcom, so I had no idea what to expect. I was eating my pizza and burger—the weekly cheat-day meal—and turned on HBO Max and scrolled. I saw Jerrod Carmichael's profile and red shirt and thought, *Why not.*

And I was stunned, moved to tears, ecstasy. In his comedy stand-up special, he discussed the various lies families tell to keep moving on, to keep going. The lies his father told his mother. The lies he held for his father. And the lie, or hidden truth, of keeping his sexual desires and pleasures from his mother. And it's not hyperbolic to say I'd never experienced a comedy special like his. I wasn't prepared—for when I'd laugh, for when I'd literally fight tears, for questions that remained when the sound of applause literally stopped but action kept moving. In a throbbingly visceral way, I was moved.

There are some lies we tell to protect others. There are others we tell to protect ourselves. *Rothaniel* explores the consequences of certain kinds of tales told and untold and what it feels like to hold and carry them.

He talked about knowing his mother's favorite Bible scripture. And if you know your mama has a favorite scripture, and you know what that scripture is, and you can even quote it, you might just be a Black church boy. The way Carmichael dealt with and in religion and spirituality felt so specific and correct. It was the first time someone described the heartbreak of hoping for a certain kind of relationship with a parent—and, specifically, a mother—that was severed when he named and refused to be ashamed of his sexuality.

His mother, he described, listened to his coming out but said, *I have to follow Jesus.* Small things can sometimes be incalculable refusals. A search for connection after truth revealed, rejected.

Peter

Long before I left Philly, I met a kid on some website. I don't recall this one either. But I loved talking to him. Sent a pic and he was short, had a Philly beard and accent, and was sweet, kind. I was a bit incredulous he wanted to meet because I didn't believe a cute short dude like him would actually find me attractive. We were both church boys trying to figure our shit out and talked openly about it. It was beautiful.

We were supposed to meet at Black Lily, a soul music gathering in the city. But I'd never been. I was still very much trying to be saved, sanctified, and filled with the Holy Ghost like the Black Pentecostal church taught me. And he had a not-yet-famous cousin who was performing and he wanted to meet there. And instead of going, I stood him up.

And I did so because what would have happened had I liked him as much in person as I did on the phone? My theology at that time could not bend or stretch enough to accommodate this sort of confrontation, so I refused it, the connection with him.

I tried reconnecting with him a couple of years ago and I don't know if he didn't remember me or if he did and didn't care, but it was clear that I had fumbled the bag—he was still cute as shit with the Sunni beard and short just like I like them. But I had to take the L.

Blake

A couple of days after I cried in Waffle House, still very heartbroken then—still am today—I called my mother as I normally do on Mondays. I was on my way to the gym, having canceled teaching earlier that day because I was still distraught. On the phone with her, after I asked how she was doing, she asked how I was and I couldn't come up with words without their meeting with tears. So, I tried. Loudly. I was at the corner of the street in the car and had to pull over. *Someone I really care about . . .* And I couldn't finish. *I am so tired of being alone.*

And there was this moment, beauty in heartbreak. *I'm lonely too,* she said, also beginning to cry. She talked about wanting connection and friendship.

And, but, then.

Maybe you can start reading your word again.

Whatever door had opened closed.

Was my heartbreak, were my tears, was this sadness an opening for conversion, for me to realize that maybe I should return to the church and get saved and recommit to a life serving Jesus as a straight or, if not straight, an abstinent man? Was my *so unbearable that even though I'd never ever in my life even mentioned interest in a man before to my mother, I could not contain it and not say anything to her* heartbreak, even if difficult, cause for celebration? Were my tears proof of answered prayer?

The silence pulsing through *Rothaniel* made absolute sense to me when he described his mother. Because he was so close to her, their relationship so intimate, but that intimacy was refused when it was suggested that Jesus takes primacy. And Jesus does for his mother. And for my mother too. I felt *Rothaniel* because I understood how the gut punch of certain throwaway statements, questions, phrases, and silences feels. Silence that says so much.

Because there was mostly silence after Waffle House too. After months of not initiating a conversation, on a Tuesday night in June while I was on the phone with my brother, he called. It'd been months since I'd heard his voice. On the other side, he was crying. I asked how he was doing. *Not good.* I asked what was wrong. *I think I'm dying,* he said. COVID had been ravaging communities for months and it was still very difficult to understand. I had to hold back my tears. And had to calm my breathing too.

Over the next half hour, I managed to calm him down; his breathing slowed, his tears subsided. *We could go to the ER but that'd risk exposure,* I said, so he took my advice and waited for urgent care the next day. He called me and told me the time of his appointment. I drove there and waited. Because of COVID, no one was being allowed into the lobby except people there to be seen by the staff. He eventually came out and we stood around the parking lot for forty minutes talking.

Thank you for calling me . . .

Thank you for coming . . .

I still care about y— . . . And I trailed off because I was there, near tears. It was good to see him. The first time in months. He would call me later, he said. But he didn't. Five days came and went before he reached out to say hello. We laughed. Shared memes. It was easing back into what it was, a relaxing, a saying yes to being moved by one another again. As we text messaged each other, I told him I had been really worried the previous week, heard the worry in his voice, was so glad he was okay.

I am as well, was his response.

lol, lowercase, I said. I did not know what to say. I still do not. So I haven't tried.

And he hasn't said a word to me since that day, a week after crying on the phone because of fear, a week after I met him at urgent care.

Ashon

This could be about my folly with dating—the funny shit that's happened, the sadness too. Because who cries in the Waffle House during the day? It wasn't the night shift and I'd stopped drinking months before, so I couldn't even blame being drunk or hungover for my tears. It's sad but, years later, also kinda funny in a terribly sick way. But this is also about the restive search for connection and the many ways we refuse it after having found it, afraid of how it will transform us. But the fear over how it *will* means it already *has*. We can retreat like parents do but that retreat is a ruse. We can stop looking at the pictures, stop visiting the social media pages, but the desire that prompted such looking and visiting will remain.

The Necessary Changes Have Been Made

＊

NAFISSA THOMPSON-SPIRES

Though he had theretofore resisted the diminutive form of his name, in his new office Randolph felt, for the first time, like a Randy.

If Randolph were truthful, he could admit that he began acting like a Randy months before Isabela and especially the week before the holiday. That Tuesday, after Isabela had wished him a tepid "Happy Thanksgiving" and he was sure she was gone for the week-end, Randolph had picked up the little silver picture frame on her desk and spit-washed her face and meager breasts through the glass, swirling his index finger until she blurred into a mucoid uni-boob. He returned the frame, packed his things into two blue copy-paper boxes, and shuttled them to his new office, hoping his bonsai would survive the transition and the dark holiday. Even with the lamps he purchased, the room was dim, but he was determined to keep the fluorescents off. His new office sat at the back of a musty corner near the janitorial closet, but it was, he reassured himself, *his* musty corner. He drove home for the break pleased with his victory and the progress and restraint he showed in achieving it.

Before Isabela, DIY had been the subject of Randolph's irritation, and before DIY, Crystal, before Crystal, Fatima, and before Fatima,

Randolph's mother, the Virgin Mary, and a girl who sneered at him in second grade.

Before Isabela, when Randolph was first hired at Wilma Rudolph, an HBCU, the department chair, Carol, had introduced him to Dr. Ivan-Yorke, saying that he should meet with her at least twice during the semester so that she could provide a letter for his file. Other than the fact that Randolph and DIY were two of the only three Black professors in the department, he wasn't sure why he was assigned to Ivan-Yorke. She didn't work in his specialization and hadn't written anything of note in decades. Her eyes sat high on her head and deep in her face, which, because of its plumpness, reminded Randolph of gingerbread dough. Randolph had seen her the day of his interview limping down the narrow hallway in what he described later to his friend Reggie as some sort of funereal muumuu but which at the time struck him as a plain black dress.

"This is Dr. Randolph Green, a new assistant professor," Carol had said, "from Preston." Dr. Ivan-Yorke glared coolly down her square glasses before lifting her head slightly and gesturing for Randolph to examine the collection of office mugs displayed on her shelves. Randolph's glance—for he was astute at times—picked up a DIY theme. One mug, lavender with white lettering, said, KEEP CALM AND DO IT YOURSELF. Another said, A JOB IS NEVER DONE UNTIL I'VE DONE IT. Carol looked at him apologetically, laughing a little. "That's right. I forgot to tell you that everyone here calls Dr. Ivan-Yorke 'DIY.' Her favorite saying is—"

"Do it yourself," DIY interrupted, with one flaccid arm raised toward her collection.

"Ha," Randolph forced.

"Come closer," DIY whispered. "I've been here for over twenty years."

There was no one in the hallway or the nearby offices. Randolph didn't understand why she spoke so quietly.

"I've read some of your work," DIY mouthed. "Why did you leave the prestigious Preston?"

"You know," Randolph said. "Wanted to try something different." He didn't say what he told others: that he wanted a reprieve from performing his status as an antistereotype or that he needed a break from the beneficence of liberal guilt, all eyes on him, the expectations of smiling, gesturing women. He felt one of his migraines already. They started in the small indentation at the base of his head, where neck meets pituitary cavity. The veins constricted as though a nylon cable were forcing the blood up, up, and out of his forehead. Pressure flooded the ocular nerves, concentrating itself behind one eye or the flat bone around his temple. He saw no aura, only felt the violence of it all.

"You know how it is," Randolph repeated.

"I don't," DIY said, turning back to her desk.

Carol and Randolph saw themselves out of the office.

Randolph hadn't wanted to share an office any more than he'd wanted to teach at a historically Black university, but Wilma Rudolph was the only other university in the city and was the only one still looking for an advanced assistant professor in the late spring, and by then he'd have done anything to get away from Preston and what he and Reggie called its "tyranny of whiteness." It turned out, to Randolph's dismay, that while the students at Wil U were mostly Black, the faculty was nearly as homogeneous as Preston's, especially in the humanities. The school, he felt, was run almost entirely by women, and Randolph came to understand them as an unholy sisterhood of pseudofeminists, with DIY as their unofficial leader, Carol their henchwoman-in-training, and Isabela their likely successor. A Black man, he told Reggie, was just as much a token there as on the other side of the city.

The consolation prize for the job was his double office with the most enviable windows in the building. The other nontenured faculty members were housed in two slums on the third and fourth floors of the building, sitting five or six people to spaces that should have been called carrels. But the two faculty members who'd shared the office previously had left on short notice, bequeathing to Randolph a large, well-lit space of his own. Until Isabela.

She was hired in late September, a month into the school year, after the department chair of Spanish and Portuguese received complaints from students that their class was unassigned to an instructor. A professor from the Spanish department walked into Randolph's office with a woman at her side, gestured toward the partition and second desk, and told Isabela, "This will be yours," before she introduced herself and Randolph's new office mate. Isabela smiled in a way that most people, including Randolph, would perceive as warm, and asked his department.

"English, literature really." Randolph smiled back.

"Oh, good. You will help me. I'm from Venezuela. My writing in English is not so good."

"Well, neither is my Spanish," he said with a laugh.

"This is my first time teaching in the States," she said. "I taught in Venezuela."

"It's my first time teaching at an HBCU, too." Randolph wanted to make that clear.

"It's a beautiful campus, very green," she said.

"It's a campus," he said.

She smiled and nodded for a reason Randolph couldn't interpret, then began to unpack the little rolling suitcase she had brought. Randolph showed her where to find office supplies, how to adjust the thermostat, which had a tendency to stick, and how to sign up for the university's text-alert system. At Preston, crimes on or near campus were summarized in a monthly email from PR, probably to minimize the sense of widespread criminality, though the numbers were likely similar to Wil U's. At Wil U, crimes were part of the daily tableau. Alert: reported sexual assault on the fourth floor of Wiley. Alert: students robbed outside McGill. Alert: black Mitsubishi Gallant stolen from West Featherringhill parking lot. Sometimes students sounded like they were going to fight in the hallway. Once, two faculty members did. The anxiety didn't even register for Randolph anymore, he said, but he thought Isabela, especially as a woman, should be prepared.

Isabela, however, seemed almost unfazed as Randolph told her the stories. She nodded, her eyes serious as he spoke. "The school where I taught in Caracas is very violent."

"Hmm," he said. "Where I grew up was rough, but I didn't expect it at a university, even one in the South or in the hood." He put the word in scare quotes. "Ghetto?" he asked, unsure if she understood.

She shrugged and twisted her lips, as if to say she'd expected it. "People are the same, where you put them."

Randolph shrugged this time. He finished the tour of the office by telling Isabela that he liked to keep the lights off because of a sensitivity to artificial light and, he emphasized, because of the great windows in the room. The office faced south and was fully lit until the late afternoon most days, the trees outside providing just enough shade so that the sun never felt sharp. She nodded slowly, her lips pursed. He continued, "We can close the office door if things get too loud in the hall."

Randolph realized as soon as the words left his mouth their potential for misinterpretation. He should probably keep the office door open, for her sake, for the sake of propriety. He watched her face for discomfort and found none. Still, he started to explain that he hadn't meant anything, but she just said, "Yes, I don't like lots of noise."

He thought they would be friends. They were about the same age, unmarried and content with that status. Randolph didn't want to date another coworker, and Isabela, he said, wasn't his type anyway, though Randolph's friends would say that wasn't true. He wouldn't even meet with his former coworkers at the Preston campus, for fear of running into his ex Crystal, a history professor who said that Randolph's passivity belied chauvinism and that his book proposal, *The New New Paternalism: Romantic Racism and Sexism in the Post-Postracial Era,* would continue to go nowhere until he confronted his own masculinity issues. Crystal confused Randolph, because she wanted him to be angrier, scarier in bed, bought him books on erotic asphyxiation, called him Smaller Thomas during an argument, and concluded that he had low T, but broke up with him after he got "too rough." She couldn't have it both ways, he argued. "You always overcorrect or undercorrect, but never get it just right," she cried.

When describing Isabela, then, Randolph oversold her undesirable aspects: She was not unattractive, but flat, bland yet aggressive. She wore her brown hair in a ponytail, which accentuated her ears. All her features were tiny—her ears like those of a little old man, and her nose, a narrow point with a slightly beaked end—yet overpronounced.

Isabela, he later learned, wanted to settle into life in the United States, maybe find a tenure-track job, before dating. It was a perfect situation for maintaining a platonic relationship, which Randy insisted he wanted. They both felt underdressed among the students, who alternated between church and club wear to classes. They laughed easily. She ate trail mix from a Ziploc bag. Randolph ate granola mixed with M&M's. They kept their respective desks tidy and arranged their bric-a-brac just so. They shared disbelief at their students' general boldness.

One rainy day in mid-October, Isabela sighed, a bit dramatically, Randolph thought. She must have had an altercation with a student, but when he asked, she said, "Randy, it is very dark in here today. May I turn on the lights?"

Randolph considered how to answer. He didn't want this to become a pattern. "Oh," he said. "Well, remember, I keep them off because I can't deal with the fluorescent bulbs. I get migraines." He pointed to his chestnut-colored forehead and frowned.

She nodded. "Yes, but it is very dark."

"It's fine today, I guess. I'm leaving soon, but in general, I prefer not to have them on." Randolph fiddled with his necktie.

She turned on the lights. The department chair, Carol, stepped into the office as Randolph packed up his bag.

"Oh, Randolph, I'm glad I caught you," she said, her face flushed, though it always looked that way. "I was going to email you, but I was walking by the office anyway. Dr. Ivan-Yorke says you two haven't officially met for a mentoring session. Remember you need to meet twice each semester. I wouldn't wait too long. You know how it is after the break."

"I'll get on that." Randolph fake smiled.

"Great. Hi, Isabela," Carol said before she left. "How're you liking the office?"

"It is very nice with the lights on," she said, looking at Randolph.

Carol paused and, glancing at Randolph, said, "I suppose it would be."

Randolph didn't know what to make of Isabela's comment at the time, so he focused on Carol's. He'd avoided his mentoring meetings because DIY struck him as another nut among many in the school's canister. Though he was six feet three, he felt something shrink in her presence.

A few days after the first time she requested more light, on a day that Randolph did not recall as particularly overcast, Isabela beat him into the office, and when he arrived all the lights were on. He sat down at his desk and considered how he should approach the situation. Perhaps she didn't understand the severity of his medical problems. He could call her over to his desk and pull up a Wikipedia page about migraines. He could say, in Spanish, that he really preferred natural light to all this fake stuff, which changes the rhythm of the brain and disrupts work. He could tell her that he'd been generous by using headphones, instead of speakers, to listen to music, so the least she could do was let him leave the lights off.

He said, pantomiming an expansive space, "The windows are very big, bright, don't you think?"

She said, "Yes, but an office without lights? It is very strange. It doesn't look nice."

"What about a desk lamp?"

"Desk lamp." She spit the words out like they were made of metal.

"It's a little light that sits on your side of the office, for overcast days."

"I know what it is. I will think about it," she said, turning back to her computer. She did not offer to turn off the lights. "It is cold in here," she said, pulling her sweater around her chest.

When Reggie called Randolph that afternoon to check on him, Randolph tried to describe the environment accurately, starting with DIY.

"She's at least seventy and limps along the hallways with a cane, flashing warnings at visible and invisible offenses. She's not the department chair, but you'd think so," he said.

"Sounds like Black Crazy personified," Reggie said, though he said that about nearly anyone he saw as overworked, and about most female academics who happened to be Black. Reggie had served as Randolph's assigned faculty mentor at Preston through the Minority Mentoring Program. He was about ten years older than Randolph, and had written a book called *Black Crazy: Tipping Points in Black Literature, 1874–1974.* He took Randolph to lunch once a month, observed his classes a few times, and wrote a recommendation letter that would sit in his Interfolio queue should Randolph choose "not to fool around after this little experiment is over and get a real job at a research university."

"She's Black Crazy all right. I'll tell you about her later. But look, Reg, I want to pick your brain about my new office mate."

He described Isabela as "a wall with a nose," hoping to avoid a lecture.

"Good. I've told you before—"

Reggie repeated his stock advice, the same advice Randolph's parents and all his other mentors, formal and informal, repeated: "Don't screw it up. Err on the side of passivity. Don't date anyone in the humanities departments. Don't even look at those women's legs when they pull out their short skirts in the spring or when they prance up the stairs in those leggings." Lost in his lecture, Reggie failed to give Randolph any useful suggestions about the light situation.

Randolph assured him that there was no chance of him dating Isabela and said goodbye. Before he hung up, he heard an incredulous "Mhhhm," though Randolph supposed he could see why Reggie wouldn't believe him. At Preston, Randolph had broken two of Reggie's rules at once by dating Crystal—both colleague and white woman—and a third when he told him he wanted to take a break from the research setting and get a teaching job at a liberal arts school for a couple of years. "You're on your way to Black Crazy," Reggie said with a shrug. "If your students don't kill you, the four-four load will."

The teaching load was heavier than Randolph expected, even after hearing Reggie's stories of lost colleagues and "scholars who showed so much promise early on," but the environment bothered Randolph the most, the cramped classrooms, the oldness of the place, its sharp luminance. In meetings, Randolph pouted while DIY sat on her elevated chair whispering, the women leaning in, straining to hear her. That's how they all were, Randolph concluded, making you lean into them and accommodate their every whim, their eccentricities. Randolph had begun to hate the whole lot of them.

When he returned to his office—their office—after class the next day, the door was open and the lights were on. Randolph thwacked his folder and a stack of papers on his desk without looking at Isabela.

"You can turn the lights off," she said without looking up. She was wearing one of those sweaters with a low-cut oval neck that usually look good on really skinny girls, yet somehow it did not, Randolph insisted, look good on Isabela.

"Oh, no," he said. "It's fine."

"No, I did not know if you were gone for the day or for a class. It's okay." She frowned, nodding toward the light switch.

"I'm only going to be here for a few more minutes. It's fine."

Randolph fumbled through his desk drawer for a bottle of Aleve and his prescription pills, looking from one bottle to the other, as if making a decision about which level of migraine he had. He rattled the pills around and poured one into his hand. He could feel her mouth mocking him, even with her head turned, her little beak scrunching up.

"It's a real condition, you know," Randolph started, loudly, "over-illumination. I literally get headaches from these lights, all fluorescent lights."

"Hmm."

He pointed to his head. "You've never had a migraine, I guess."

"No. It's okay, turn off the light."

Randolph asked his three o'clock class how they would deal with "an inconsiderate roommate who, for instance, made a lot of noise while you were trying to sleep."

Someone said, "Mind games."

Another said, "Man, I'd tell him to keep it down. When I gotta study, I don't have time to play."

"Just ask for another roommate," someone else said.

"Like that would work," several people seemed to say at once.

On Monday, he got up twenty minutes early to beat Isabela into the office. When she came in, she smiled and said hello as though nothing had changed between them. Randolph made small talk, taking the opportunity to build a bridge, if a bridge is defined as the path to getting one's own way.

"Would you like me to get you the desk lamp?" he started. "You know, this was my idea, and I feel bad about adding an expense. I can buy the lamp." That sounded fine, he thought, not too pushy, but hopefully rhetorically manipulative enough to remind her of the gravity of the situation.

"That is fine." Her mouth went from neutral to something else. They didn't speak again that day.

The morning Randolph presented her with the lamp, in what he hoped was a cute mosaic pattern, Isabela did not smile. She paused with tight lips and said, "Thank you," leaving the lamp untouched.

She beat him to the office for the next couple of weeks and turned on all the lights except her desk lamp. Whenever one left, the other adjusted the lighting to his or her preference. Randolph researched overillumination, looking for ways to convince Isabela of her insensitivity. Two of the friends he polled said he was making a big deal out of nothing; she probably just didn't understand. Two other friends said she was being a jerk, and there was no way she could misunderstand. Jerry, a mutual friend of Reggie's, said, "This is the kind of petty drama that can only happen with a woman. She's the aggressor, but watch out now, or she'll make it all look like your fault." Reggie said this was about power and that Randolph could only lose, whichever way he played it. If he acted aggressively, he became what "they" always knew he would be, and she won. If he let her have the office, she won. "How do you think I went from Reginald to Reggie?" he said. "You can't win, brother." The Richter needles in Randolph's temples charted small hills.

What else could Randolph do? He'd tried reasoning and compromise. He fantasized about driving Isabela out of the office, delighting in her expression at the sight of a fake rat spinning in her chair or a Spanish-English dictionary on her desk. He'd seen people on reality television rub their testicles on their housemates' mattresses or pillowcases and brush the inner rim of a toilet with their toothbrushes. The victims never found out until they met for the reunion episodes and watched the footage together. Randolph wasn't ready to pull his balls out over this, nor did he like the way they could implicate him in a potential misreading of the situation, but he thought about it.

One late morning while she was still in class, Randolph went over to Isabela's desk and flattened the bag of trail mix she always kept there, crunching a few of the nuts with his thumb and watching their oil streak the plastic. As quickly as he could, he removed all but a few of the yogurt-covered raisins and put them into his pants pocket. He flicked the desk lamp on and off three times and returned to his desk to eat the raisins before they melted into a mess, the cream and hydrogenated oils thick and sweet against his gums.

When he returned from class, Isabela was out of the office, and a book called *Microaggressions* had been left on Randolph's desk. He tossed the book to her side of the office, not caring where it landed. When he pulled his lunch bag out of his desk drawer, he found his sandwich spotted with four abnormally large dimples on each side of the bread, like deep fingerprints. Randolph removed the bread from his sandwich, placed it back into the paper bag, and ate the smoked turkey directly from the plastic.

At his urban middle school in Chicago, a kid was shot for allegedly stealing someone's lunch. At Wil U, a faculty member was caught going through another one's desk drawers, and a fistfight broke out in the hallway. The woman won. At Wil U, a boy had been jumped for leaving the library at the wrong time. At Preston, Randolph found that people with money committed these assaults but left fewer traces, the violence psychological. He heard stories of girls saturating tampons with ketchup and sticking them into other girls' thousand-dollar handbags. They published anonymous glossy newsletters accusing male professors of roving eyes or worse and tucked them into faculty mailboxes. Caracas or not, Isabela didn't know how Randolph's dual schooling had prepared him to get ugly. She didn't know with whom she was fooling.

In fact, Randolph would call his problem one of duality, twoness, though not in the purely Du Boisian sense, but in the sense that he was of two minds about most things, and very few of those things converged. He maintained two social media pages, one for colleagues and one for old friends who knew him when. Both included the phrase "it's complicated" under his name. Reggie would say that the tyranny of whiteness both emasculated him and expected him to adopt hypermasculinity. Randolph could find no nonbinary position on the continuum. He could only flip-flop.

Randolph didn't tell Reggie about his sandwich or the raisins, but he told him that the migraines were getting worse, even with the dose of amitriptyline he'd been prescribed. Reggie said, "Those headaches will go away once you stop feeling like you have to be some kind of standard, once you just let it all out. The problem is once you do that, you won't have a job. For me it's nosebleeds. I call 'em my monthly cycle. The pressure has to come out some kind of way."

.   .   .

On a Tuesday, while Isabela and the lights were out, Randolph sneaked over, again, to her side of the office. She had apparently hidden the trail mix, because it was not in sight. In the silver-framed picture on her desk, she hugged her toddler nephew and wore a red cocktail dress. Randolph fingered the floral-print cup that held her collection of number 2 pencils, most of them yellow and sheathed in those soft cushions that slide over the top. He pulled the sheath off one of the pencils and squished it around in his hand. The pencils were freshly sharpened, the goldenrod, brown, and black contrasting attractively. Randolph took a sheet of Isabela's scratch paper, then used each pencil in succession, dulling the lead by pressing hard as he drew little spirals, each stroke of the pencil a little ecstasy. He hid the blackened paper in his messenger bag and removed any dust or traces of broken points that had landed on the desk and rearranged the pencils as he remembered them. He didn't want to be the next blip on the text-alert system. Alert: robbery and assault in office of non-tenure-track female faculty member. Suspect: tall Black male, generally thought handsome, accused of keeping the lights off in a suggestive manner, eating fourteen yogurt-covered raisins, and breaking a desk lamp and eleven pencils.

He returned to his own desk, locking up the blackened scratch paper, his lunch, and all his office supplies. He noted the spot where the blue edge of his bonsai's pot lined up with the silver crack in the file cabinet.

The Monday before Thanksgiving, Randolph arranged a mentoring meeting with DIY, hoping to feel her out about the potential for a new office. He planned to discuss his upcoming annual review and then to casually bring up the situation with Isabela. He knocked and stepped into the office carefully, but she whispered, "Just have a seat. You don't need all that false formality with me. How is your semester going?"

"It's okay, an adjustment."

She watched Randolph's face too carefully, for too long, before she said, "You don't like that office mate, do you?"

Randolph laughed, debating whether he should tell her the truth, unsure what she would do with it. "I just don't want to make her uncomfortable," he started, and felt compelled to apologize for this dishonesty, "but actually she's making me uncomfortable." DIY didn't stir. He looked away from her eyes; their cloudiness reminded him of marbles you might trade away. "You're a woman," he began again, feeling like a liar, for her femaleness seemed, to him, buried far beneath the nest of thinning hair, the severe black clothes. "I don't want it to look bad, you know, like I'm doing some kind of exercise in male domination." He chuckled.

DIY made a *pfff* noise with her mouth and leaned back before she leaned in. She took deep inhalations from the back of her throat and exhaled the words without parting her teeth. "That's your problem," she said. "You're afraid of the light."

He started to speak, but she gave him a withering look.

"You think you're too good for this school. It's obvious to me. You don't want to be exposed, so you overcorrect in some places, but it all comes out somewhere else."

"I don't think I follow," Randolph said, the word "overcorrect" pinching his ego.

"That's one of your other problems." She paused her rebuke for a moment before trying again. "There's this saying in law, 'mutatis mutandis,' 'the necessary changes have been made.' It doesn't apply to you."

"And how exactly is this relevant?" The veiled hints and analogies were too much for Randolph's migraine.

"Sometimes the problem is the environment; sometimes you *are* the environment. In your case, you think you're making changes, but you take the problem with you, like you did exchanging your old job for this one." She gestured with one hand for him to leave.

Randolph left the meeting furious with DIY, though he couldn't put his finger on exactly why. He asked Carol about the new office that day, and though it looked like another demotion of sorts, it represented, for him, a battle he won, growing a pair.

·   ·   ·

As he walked out of a faculty meeting one wintry afternoon, Randy paused near the adjunct who'd moved in with Isabela, a skinny guy with adult acne. "How do you like the new office?"

"It's good," he said. "Nice windows."

"Why do you guys have the lights off? Are you a migraine sufferer?"

"No, Isabela's idea," the adjunct said. "She gets really hot, so she keeps them off. You know, boiler's right under us."

Dancing in the Dark

✳

CLOVER HOPE

I don't know what made me think I could move like Janet Jackson, but I know I tried. In spring 1995, Janet and her brother Michael released what was then (and still is) the most expensive music video ever made ($7 million): a hyperfuturistic, black-and-white visual for their angry duet "Scream," from Michael's ninth studio album. In the video, the two are on a spaceship screaming about injustice. Then comes the breakdown. The beat fades as they dramatically approach the camera and drop to their knees in one smooth motion. You know it's about to go down. They hop back up to their feet in sync, then crisscross and drop to their knees again. I didn't try any of that. I didn't have the knees for it, even at twelve years old. What I mimicked was the simplest part of the routine: a swinging arm motion. That's it.

This process of learning choreography from music videos became a regular practice for me in the privacy of my childhood attic in Jamaica, Queens. Back in the days of music television, I'd watch choreo breakdowns on BET, MTV, or Ralph McDaniels's *Video Music Box*. (Queens natives might also remember a local music video program hosted by a guy named Bobby. I'm not sure if he ever had a last name. I just remember him as "Bobby.") From TLC's shoulder shimmy in the "Waterfalls" video to Brandy's Bankhead Bounce, it was all part of the essential training that would carry me through a life of chronically self-aware public dancing-while-Black.

The struggle to dance adequately followed me throughout my youth, college, and twentysomething years until I realized how well alcohol could quell my anxieties. It's a good question when you think about it: How exactly do we even learn? I mean, people. More specifically, Black people. The existential answer is that Black people have it *in* us. The belief is that we all have some kind of Tony Stark arc reactor inside, bestowed by the ancestors, that allows us to bop on the one and three. In reality, we don't just wake up one day and suddenly start body-rolling like inflatable tubes at gas stations. At the least, most of us have the first step down: understanding the basic concept of rhythm. Some access it better or more quickly than others. And more often than not, we learn from observation. Hence my attempts at choreography.

It didn't help growing up in a household of nondancers. We didn't throw parties, though looking back, I did dance with reckless abandon around the house because that's what you do when you're younger. I was born in Guyana and came to America with my parents when I was about one year old. In addition to Caribbean staples like reggae, calypso, and soca, my dad would play vinyl records by everyone from Whitney Houston and Madonna to Stevie Wonder, MC Hammer, and all the Motown oldies but goodies, teaching me about different genres before I really even understood what they were. We were immigrants discovering popular American music and, frequently, Black American musicians. Music had a presence in our house, so there was always a melody in my heart. But that was in the comfort of my home. Plus, when you're young, you mostly do silly arm flails, not consciously moving to the beat. (My theory is that some part of white people's brains never advances past this stage. I believe their dance growth is stunted in that way. In essence, they are always "young-dancing.") Public dancing is a whole other thing.

As an adolescent, I didn't have access to the rhythm in my bones yet. I remember going to barbecues and seeing other families do the Electric Slide, which I think I learned in school somehow. And there were attempts to push me in the right direction—some invisible force likely guiding my mother toward putting my older sister and me into dance classes at a local organization, Charosa. There, I took ballet, tap, and the generic category hip-hop. I can't remember ever being "good" in those classes. The real turning point for my dance education was basement and backyard parties.

In my neighborhood, you'd hear about parties through these things called flyers, which were printed on paper and posted around the block on trees at a time when computers were still for rich people. Or through word of mouth you'd hear that someone was throwing a summer bash. I would either beg my mom to let me attend or not tell her. I keenly remember parties at three locations: Trevor and Craig's backyard (brothers who lived on the block perpendicular to mine); the basement of a boy named Raymond; and the backyard of a school friend, Ericka, whom I later reunited with in adulthood.

To set the scene for these parties, I have to talk about the soundtrack of the nineties, when most of what was blasting out of cars and radios was by Puff Daddy and his Bad Boy Entertainment slate. Puffy was spinning in videos, and on any given day, you'd hear a then-unordained Ma$e screaming, "Do that Puff Daddy shit!" from the ether. It was a time of Biggie and Tupac, Dr. Dre and Snoop Dogg, Total and 112. Wu-Tang Clan, Outkast, Salt-N-Pepa, Jay-Z. Missy Elliott, Aaliyah, and Timbaland. Brandy, Xscape, Mariah Carey. Basically, a golden era of hip-hop and R & B where I simply could not flee the rhythm. And so I stopped *trying to dance,* and I just danced.

There's a difference between choosing not to dance and dancing off-beat, by the way. I'd rather paste myself to a wall than be caught completely missing the rhythm. (Of course, we all have moments where it takes a few seconds to catch the beat, but I'm not counting those. Once you catch it, it's like swag-surfing.)

Before the dawn of "Back That Azz Up," three songs got me going at parties. First was the Ghost Town DJs' classic "My Boo." Once I heard that angelic acoustic intro and the 808s dropped, (subtle) bedlam ensued. I'm not saying I was body-rolling that well. Twerking wasn't a trend yet. But there, in that basement, I learned to grind. As a product of West Indies culture, slow-winding was fused into my DNA, ready for me to access. But it's one thing to see people winding their waists in videos or at adult parties and think you can mimic them. It's another thing to actually execute the motion and make your virgin hips do that circular grind effectively without looking stupid. I tried and was somewhat successful. To become a true slow-wind authority of the likes of Rihanna would take years of practice and sex.

Another song was 112's "Only You"—but only the superior remix, featuring Biggie. When that song came on, I would stop whatever I was doing—which was usually nothing because I wasn't talking to anyone—and push up on the nearest guy. Nothing wild. Just swaying my hips side to side to the beat. This is when I started to understand motion. The caveat was that it had to be dark so that no one could see me. I wasn't about to be throwing it back in full fluorescent light. Third, there was Next's "Too Close." I had just turned fourteen years old when their single about dry-humping in the club dropped. There was RL, singing about dudes getting excited on the dance floor. And there I was learning anatomy.

Soon, those neighborhood parties became more infrequent, and friends began to disappear into their future lives. But that's how I tapped into the necessary element of dance: the feeling of freedom. You can observe all you want and try to emulate what you see until it becomes ingrained. But something has to imbue you with the desire to move when you get the chance. Despite that early dance training, I was still extremely nervous about dancing in the light where everyone could see. At my high school prom, I mostly sat at the table and watched everyone, content to just bop my head. I got up a couple of times to do micro two-steps on the dance floor, but I remember the flush of heat and embarrassment I felt inside, thinking every step I made was being scrutinized.

Some people can dance in public and not feel self-conscious. And then there's the rest of us, which is why lighting was crucial at those dank basement parties. I wasn't drinking, so I couldn't use that as fuel. I wasn't a natural dancer, per se, but I've always loved music, so I probably would have found my way to the dance floor. Dancing is where I could be invisible and free. But the idea of dancing "like no one's watching" is a saying precisely because it's nerve-racking when people are watching. Will they clown you because you don't have the right meter and cadence? Will they tell their friends about it? "She couldn't even Electric Slide."

The Electric Slide is a dance tradition that breeds embarrassment across the country. Bunny Wailer, the Jamaican singer-songwriter who performed with Bob Marley and the Wailers, wrote the original "Electric Boogie" in 1976. At the time, the New York club Vamp's Disco was about to reopen, and choreographer Ric Silver was tapped to create a dance routine for it. The result was the Electric Slide we know and fear today. The problem, as with any popular line dance, is that you cannot disengage from the Electric Slide at a party. It's the type of dance that summons you. (It's literally electric.) You stand out like the person who wears color to a white party if you don't join the line.

The thing about the Electric Slide is that it's easy to forget the order of the moves if you're not doing it constantly at parties. I once attended a Juneteenth celebration where the Slide broke out. I attempted to move with the crowd but forgot the moves and felt my insides turn to shortbread. I'm sure others were too busy dancing to notice. In reality, no one cares. You're always a lot more critical and self-aware than anyone else ever will be. But that's not how being self-conscious works. It's neither logical nor accurate to think that everyone in the room is watching and laughing at you while you dance.

My history of learning to dance is heavily tied to a feeling of visibility. You grow accustomed to a life of invisibility, but the dance floor is a space where you rebuke the idea of being seen. Not only was I quiet, but I moved in silence. I wasn't a gesticulator and certainly not a dancer. I didn't want to be viewed as a bad dancer or seen at all, really. I didn't want to let people down, and it always felt like someone was watching. Through time and practice, I gradually let go of that inhibition. In my mid-twenties, I started cohosting birthday parties with one of my best friends, Erika, and it became an annual tradition. At these parties, I'd let loose. I remember one friend telling me, "I love it when you dance. You look free." People weren't used to seeing me that way. So when they'd see me dance, it was like all my rhythmic insides were spilling out and I turned into one of those "Beyoncé always on beat" memes.

I wish there were a statistic to confirm how many of us comprehended the idea of movement from watching *Soul Train*. As a music fanatic, I rarely missed an opportunity to catch *Soul Train* every Saturday. I wasn't going to concerts, so I turned to televised performances for entertainment. By the time I began watching, *Soul Train* had been on the air for more than two decades, initially premiering in 1970 as a local Chicago show hosted by creator Don Cornelius, a radio announcer. There was *American Bandstand,* an institution. But *Soul Train,* birthed concurrently with disco and hip-hop, was a space for Black acts to show off and shake their tail feathers on a national stage. It was a place for *dancers* to dance, and the Soul Train Line became a staple that migrated to Black parties nationwide.

Dance is release, technique, and tradition. Movement is expression. I write to express what I won't say out loud, and that's the same reason I dance. I can't quite describe what I feel when I hear Whitney Houston's "I Wanna Dance with Somebody." I can only demonstrate it through bodily motion. Hearing "Back That Azz Up," likewise, is the exact feeling of when the cosmos exploded and spread all the elements that exist into the universe and onto Earth. The rapper Common once said *Soul Train* "gave ordinary, everyday people an opportunity to express themselves."

In 2001, I entered Temple University before transferring to NYU for my sophomore year. Temple was my coming-out party, my chance to escape the introvert identity. I was so quiet that I was scared to ever be loud. But in college, I danced like no one was watching. At keg parties. Local bars where we were too underage to be but no one cared. It was the alcohol, obviously. I had my first drink, a Long Island iced tea, at seventeen. Then Corona and Smirnoff Ice gave me the 4.5-percent-alcohol courage to release my self-consciousness and embrace the dancer within. I was notorious for Crip Walking at parties. Which brings me to Usher.

The same year I started college, Usher released his third studio album, *8701,* featuring his single "U Don't Have to Call," about club-bing and dancing as therapy. It must have been kismet that this single coincided with both my social growth spurt and my greater foray into public dancing. Like any great midtempo R & B song, there's a breakdown in the middle. That's when, in the music video, Usher steps out of an elevator with a crew of guys. They do this move that looks like they're winding up a wheel. The routine includes sliding, snapping, two-stepping, and a twirl—a set of moves that requires coordination. I learned the entire choreography and would clear the floor at parties to drunkenly perform it in college. It took me back to those basement days of feeling free.

In time, I went from doing minimal movements to slow-winding at basement parties as a teenager to embracing being less self-conscious. Depending on my mood, I might still need a little liquid courage, but parties aren't nearly as much of a nuisance as they used to be. Then there are the days when I'm having a good time, and a song like Frankie Beverly & the Butlers and Maze's "Before I Let Go" starts playing. Suddenly, the chip in my head buzzes, telling me: *This song is perfectly synced for the Electric Slide.* I say a prayer that in that moment, I'll know what to do.

Mulatto Pride Turbo Boost

ANGELA NISSEL

In Los Angeles in the twenty-first century, sometimes it seems like damn near everyone under thirty is mixed-race. In the eighties, in my section of Philly, having a family with a White dad and a Black mom meant you were pretty much a freak. There were three recognized races in Southwest Philly: Black, Irish, and Italian. When we moved there, our family was known as "the redhead guy with the German last name, his Black wife, and their two children that you may think are Puerto Rican but the correct term is 'light-skinned.'"

My dad knew our family needed a hook to be accepted, so he became the alpha technology male of the street.

Every Saturday morning, he would brag to our next-door neighbor about his latest acquisition while they were washing their cars. "Yeah, I just picked up this remote control that—hold on to your hat—isn't attached by a long cord to the TV." The next thing you knew, other neighbors were pouring out of their row houses to test out our new devices. For a week after we got a refrigerator with an external ice and water dispenser, my parents' new friends came by with Slurpee-size cups, marveling at our space-age appliance.

"Wow! We're in the future," a woman I barely knew gasped in disbelief as ice magically filled her cup after she pressed the button marked specifically for ice.

My father's latest purchase was a top-loading VCR that churned as loudly as a food processor. The VCR cemented his status as Southwest Philly's Bill Gates. Even more important, it provided me with a new way to overdose on my favorite activity—sitting in front of a television alone, since I still had no friends because eight-year-olds don't care about ice or watching movies from the sixties and seventies from the comfort of their home.

Soon after we invested in an alarm system to protect our VCR, a small video rental store opened in our local strip mall. Video Tape Library. Every weekend, my father would set my brother and me free in that beautiful library. As an eight-year-old, most things in my life were decided for me, but in those narrow aisles, I got to make decisions. It was the most powerful I'd ever felt.

What will it be? Which hot new release can I talk about on Monday that will make the cool kids at school finally realize I, too, am cool? I thought as I skipped over my favorite cartoons in favor of more popular PG content.

I had finally decided on a tape with a Ralph Macchio–adjacent-looking guy when Dad called out that it was time to go. I grabbed my brother's hand and followed my dad to the counter. As my dad reached in his jeans for his wallet, the cashier suddenly stopped ringing up the videos. He glanced down quizzically at my brother and me, then back up to my father.

"Do you know whose kids these are?" the cashier asked.

"Never seen them in my life," my father said, his eyes scanning our bodies, like if he concentrated hard enough he might figure out how these two kids got by his side.

My first thought: *Why is Dad lying?* I mean, I knew adults lied, but my dad usually lied to my mom. And it was never about me. Mostly it was shit like "Yeah, I've been trying really hard to get a job."

Second thought: *Did an Acme anvil hit his head recently?* I knew from the tapes we rented in this very building that when roadrunners threw anvils off cliffs, people and coyotes got hurt. While I thought about whether I'd seen cartoon swirling stars around my dad's dome recently, the cashier leaned down to my eye level.

"Where are your parents?" he asked.

Where are my parents? Sir, if you don't think my Black ass belongs to the forty-year-old White guy I'm standing with, don't ask me questions—call the police.

Oh. One more thing about 1980s Southwest Philly: local newspapers would, in front-page headlines, often refer to our neighborhood as a "racial hotbed." That was shorthand for "KKK continues Southwest Philadelphia recruitment drive after White families welcome new interracial couple with the lovely gift of arson."

At eight years old I already knew how to sniff out questions that had even the most delicate notes of "race war tipping point." I knew, also, to avoid those questions, even if they were coming from someone as important as the guy in charge of finding the actual VCR tapes to put in our empty rental boxes. But I also knew my dad was the one who was *supposed* to answer racial questions. A White man was a magic wand in those segregated streets. I'd seen my mom achieve things none of her Black friends could—get apologies, get out of traffic tickets, return a My Little Pony without a receipt.

My dad was our own personal White Savior long before anyone could rent *The Blind Side*. And he'd lost that superpower right as this cashier was, in my mind, about to get my brother and me sent to a foster home.

"Whose kids are these?" the cashier yelled out to the entire store.

Everyone in the small video store glanced pitifully at the two lost Black kids, shrugged, and continued perusing the tape selections. The cashier stared at me and my brother with an exhausted, puzzled look I now recognize as *I don't get paid enough for this shit.*

With all corners of the store having eyeballed me, I knew I had to save myself. I had to fix my father's lie yet answer the cashier's original question in a way that wouldn't get us on the cover of the *Philadelphia Daily News*. I did this by loudly yelling at my dad, "Dad, stop! You are our dad, Dad!"

Checkmate, Cashier Man!! I just called the guy I'm standing with "Dad" three times. Who are you going to believe—the upstanding White guy with a wallet full of credit cards or the Black kid you think has been abandoned at the strip mall? As an adult, I know the answer to that question, but luckily, I didn't have to learn it back then. My father suddenly seemed to remember that I was his child.

"These are my kids, man," he said, laughing and shaking his head.

"I'm sorry. I thought, because they were . . . ," the cashier replied, his voice trailing off as he started ringing up our tapes. He gave the barcodes the same rapt attention I've seen anthropology professors give to rare caveman skulls and handed our rentals over to us without a further word. I'm not sure if his silence was out of shame, embarrassment, or anger. I did know I wasn't returning with my father next weekend. I loved how technology allowed me to watch *The Muppet Movie* twice in a row without commercials, but Kermit wasn't worth my feeling like an alien.

My father soon asked why I had suddenly lost interest in renting movies. I wasn't sure how to explain my embarrassment to him, plus, I also felt I had let my parents down. I knew from my mother's lectures that I was supposed to be proud to have a Black mother and a White dad—but a young sis just wanted to get a movie, not be stared at in a teachable moment. After school, I went back to entertaining myself with regular, programmed TV like the rest of our neighbors and their primitive corded remote controls.

Not too long after the tape store incident, I flipped the TV on. It was some kind of talk show. I'd usually keep flipping channels until I found something animated, but this guy Phil Donahue had just said "mixed-race kids."

They're talking about me! I thought.

I watched for less than a minute before realizing that, yes, they were talking about me, but it was about how I was going to stumble through life not being sure whether to be a skinhead or a strong Black woman. (And, yes—apparently, those were my only two options.)

Maybe this is why my dad loved the VCR. He could control my viewing habits and hide me from eighties programming where half the talk show topics were about mixed-race couples and their future confused-ass kids. The other half was about cults. Did my pigtail-wearing ass really deserve as much time as Satanic Panic? Those angry mofos in Phil's audience thought so.

Phil jogged through his audience toward a raised hand. A woman snatched his mic.

"What about the kids? It's just not fair to bring kids into the world who won't know who they are!!" she screeched.

"And we'll be back!" Phil said as the audience hooted and clapped.

Eff that. I ain't coming back. To Phil or the video store.

I had to find what we now call a "racial safe space." A television one because there were no actual other Puerto Rican or Puerto Rican–looking kids in our hood. I could easily find my dad on any UHF or VHS channel I stopped on. Not too many people were my mother's color, but at least she had a few—two and a half by my count: Nell Carter, Tootie, and the chunky mammy character from *Tom and Jerry* (a half point since they only showed her calves). I didn't understand they were stereotypes; I was jealous that they both had something and I had nothing. If they stocked *Mulatto Mouse* in Video Tape Library, that cashier would have understood that light-skinned kids could have White dads! I began to suspect that my brother and I were the only mixed kids alive. I plotted to sneak up on my mother to see if she'd break down and confirm my suspicion.

"Mom, where are all the other mixed kids?" I asked while she was watching the news. She didn't like being interrupted when the Action News team was on. My mother and her friends watched that newscast like they were being graded on it the next day. They all dressed their children according to the predictions of Dave Roberts, the quirky weatherman. If someone was caught in a hurricane without an umbrella, there was no pity, just admonishment. "Didn't you listen to Dave last night?"

Dave was king and the female news anchor, Lisa Thomas-Laury, was queen. The adults talked about her reports as though she called the news straight to their phones instead of delivering it to two million Philadelphians simultaneously through the television. Adult women carefully enunciated all of Lisa Thomas-Laury's syllables, never disrespecting her by referring to her casually as Lisa.

As a child, I knew not to interrupt two things on TV: *Dallas* and Lisa Thomas-Laury. But I pushed caution aside. I needed to know if my brother and I were on our own with this mixed shit.

"Lots of people are mixed," my mother said, looking at the ceiling as if she kept the mixed people's names written up there. "Like . . . uh . . . Lisa Thomas-Laury."

"She has green eyes!" I said. "She's White!"

"Who said mixed and Black people can't have green eyes?" my mother replied. "My father has blue eyes." She was right; her father did have blue eyes. It wasn't until I was much older that I realized that cloudy blue eyes aren't a color. They're cataracts. But, whatever.

After that day, I became Lisa Thomas-Laury's youngest devotee. I would gladly sit through the whole newscast to see the only other mixed person I knew. I summoned the courage to ask my mother to help me mail her a letter. We decided on a postcard since a prestigious woman like Lisa Thomas-Laury was probably too busy to open mail. I went with a simple greeting: "Hi, Mrs. Lisa Thomas-Laury. I'm mixed, too! Please reply!"

She never replied. That could have been because, as I would later find out, she was not mixed and probably had no idea what the hell my postcard meant. Or because my mom put a fake return address on our card, concerned with having a blatant lie tracked to our home by the esteemed lady with two last names.

My parents were both liars. You know, maybe Mr. Donahue was right—I was destined to be confused.

Of course, my mom didn't tell me she was lying until much later. She just let me sit and wait.

"Lisa Thomas-Laury is very busy. She'll write to you. Don't worry."

To me, every day without a reply meant that Lisa Thomas-Laury was either a bitch—*I mean, we're the only mixed women alive, she couldn't at least send me a signed headshot?*—or she hated me for outing her confused identity on a postcard. I would spiral about the possible ways she had rid herself of my unwanted postcard. Did she simply burn it or did she rip it up, then toss the shreds to the weather guy as a segue?

"Here you go, Dave! You can use this bullshit for tire traction in that snow you're going to tell us about!"

My mother soon realized I was anxious whenever the news came on. She knew what she had to do—lie one more time.

"David Hasselhoff is half Black and half White," my mother mentioned casually while we were watching *Knight Rider.* "Look at his skin! It's as tan as yours. And his hair," my mother continued. "Isn't that what your hair looks like when it rains?"

She was right. Michael Knight did have a curly almost-fro. However, I still wasn't ready to risk the rejection of an unanswered fan letter, so I decided instead that my new idol would be the subject of my first-ever Black History Month oral presentation, which Sister Danielle reluctantly informed my majority-White class we had to do.

"Last month, Martin Luther King gets a holiday, now this," I overheard one mom say to another at school pickup.

After sixteen consecutive Black History oral reports on the only Black people covered in our history books—Martin Luther King and Rosa Parks—Sister Danielle expanded the criteria: we could also write about important people who were friends with historical Black Americans. The last day of February, I fidgeted in my seat as Tina Campolongo, the most popular girl in the room, gave a stellar Black history report on Abraham Lincoln. It was terrifying enough reading in front of the entire class without having to follow the Emancipation Proclamation done partly as a football cheer.

I took a deep breath before taking my place at the front of the classroom. I paced myself and held my head high as I rattled off two minutes and thirty seconds of David Hasselhoff trivia. Finally, I hit my last paragraph: "Like me, David Hasselhoff has a German last name and a Black mother."

Half the class burst into laughter. Rather than wait for them to settle down, I zoomed through the last sentences of my report.

"*Knight Rider* is a great show. It comes on channel six at eight p.m. The end."

Sister Danielle asked if anyone had any questions for me. Tony, the class bully, who was later expelled for breaking into the church and stealing a tape recorder, waved his hand so hard his whole body shook in his seat.

"Knight Rider's not part Black!" Tony called out.

"That's not a question, Tony," Sister Danielle snapped. "Phrase it as a question."

"Why would you lie and say Knight Rider is Black?" Tony asked.

His face turned bright purple, and his lips twisted like he was restraining himself from punching me for sullying the sacred name of Michael Knight and his self-aware Pontiac.

"My mother said he is," I replied.

We were still at the age when we respected our parents. Whatever they said was law, so Tony had no choice but to accept that I was right until he got home to ask his parents if my mother was wrong. Then he could return the next day and bully the shit out of me. But that day, I walked to my desk with the cool kids thinking I had something in common with a prime-time small-screen star.

As I took my seat, Sister approached me with her grading pen and wrote out an A. In addition to my five minutes of popularity, I'd aced my first-ever Black History report.

After writing down my grade, Sister leaned over and whispered in my ear. "Knight Rider. That's the fellow with all the gold chains who pities the fool, right?"

I nodded enthusiastically. I wasn't giving back my A. More than that, I recall that moment as being my first understanding of why my parents sometimes lied about race. It's exhausting constantly being an unpaid on-call teacher—especially with complex issues of race. To get your passing grade—or your videotapes or time to yourself to watch the local news—sometimes, you just gotta take advantage of someone's ignorance and make some shit up.

A Real Actual Text Thread About Real Actual White Presidents with Names Like Real Actual Niggas

SAIDA GRUNDY, PANAMA JACKSON, AND DAMON YOUNG

SAIDA GRUNDY: Y'all know the nigga name is joseph ROBINETTE biden??

robinette. like the head usher.

DAMON YOUNG: That's really a nigga name

SG: like when jill gets mad she be like "NOW DONT BE LIKE THAT NETTA"

DY: Almost as nigga as William Jefferson Clinton

SG: i'm DEFINITELY calling him Netta

PANAMA JACKSON: yeah. I remember when I first heard his full name

SG: well william jefferson clinton either owns slaves or was one

PJ: a lot of presidents had black names if you think about it.

ulysses grant. thomas jefferson.

SG: i mean only other ulysses out here is niggas. grover cleveland. how that nigga NOT play sax??

PJ: chester arthur

franklin pierce

RUTHERFORD B MOTHERFUCKING HAYES

DY: Shit, Gerald Ford. How many white Geralds you know?

PJ: all the best Geralds are definitely Black.

    Woodrow Wilson.

    Millard Fillmore definitely freebases in Bmore

    this is a piece Damon. "Quite a Few Presidents Have Black Names."

SG: please lead with Robinette tho. bc NOBODY is out here creeping with a 63 yr old black secretary's name

DY: ulysses grant is definitely a philandering usher at 7th baptist

PJ: Damon Young throws block party; Rutherford B Hayes and Millard Fillmore from East Liberty Had Big Fun.

PJ: I've actually been looking over the names of former presidents and I can't decide whose name is the Blackest. Calvin Coolidge (who was born John Calvin Coolidge Jr. but changed it so he could have a jazz name) or Gerald Rudolph Ford Jr.

    Though obviously, Rutherford B. Hayes and Ulysses S. Grant are strong contenders. Something about the name Calvin levels up the Blackness. There could be a Calvin Coolidge today and there would be absolutely no doubt that it would be a Black football-playin' nigga.

SG: RUTHERFORD mahnigga. and the only other ulysses i know is morehouse from houston

    joseph ROBINETTE biden!

    rutherford hayes. brother of isaac.

PJ: Thing is, you wouldn't even know about Joe's middle name unless you found out. Calvin Coolidge my nigga. That nigga manages a McDonald's in Newark right now. Ain't no more Rutherfords.

    I just googled "niggas named Rutherford" crickets

DY: Biden is the only president with a hairdresser from Memphis's middle name

PJ: So, that nigga Grover Cleveland's real name is Stephen Grover Cleveland and Stephen Cleveland sounds like he does the 3–7 radio show

    I wonder if there were too many stevie clevelands so he was like they gon call me Grover

DY: Frankie Lymon's second wife's name-ass nigga. Who the fuck would choose Grover over Stephen? Had quaaludes been invented yet?

PJ: this is my question.

also, Franklin Pierce just usurped all the Blackness

this white nigga's middle name is Kendrick. He is Franklin Kendrick Pierce

that's just like William Jefferson Clinton

also, Kendrick up there hated niggas

SG: franklin pierce literally the name of a limited edition GT cruiser

PJ: We should rank these niggas names for Blackness

hold the phone. We're actually looking at the wrong list. The VPs names are also nigga-rish

There's a Levi Morton

Hannibal Hamlin

SG: played bass for the max roach quartet, yes

PJ: William Wheeler (you know they called him Willie Wheeler . . . and THAT is a niggas name)

SG: rollin ray rolled so willie wheeler could wheel

PJ: nigga there is LITERALLY a VP named George Clinton

SG: he painted the white house. . . . . ?

DY: Willie Wheeler is a shortstop for the Homestead Grays—"Fast" Willie

PJ: which is also how he likes his women

DY: In 1932 he stole 52 bases and the owner's wife

Then he allegedly stabbed a mailman in Newark

Life with Eddie and Martin is loosely based off his life

SG: whistlin willie wheeler—pitched a perfect game against the birmingham black barons

PJ: Don't forget Levi Morton—"Lookin'" Levi Morton

Cuz he looks at your girl and looks off batters.

DY: Thomas Jefferson, George Washington, Andrew Jackson, Zachary Taylor, James Madison, James Monroe, John Tyler, James K. Polk, William Henry Harrison, Andrew Johnson, Martin Van Buren, Ulysses S. Grant—these are the slave owning presidents.

Zach Taylor and Martin Van Buren are the only ones who don't sound overtly black.

PJ: I know a nigga named Zachary Taylor. he had a brother named Yrachaz

DY: Wut.

PJ: Which is yes, Zachary backward. I went to school with them.

DY: I knew of a woman named lufituaeb—beautiful spelled backward

SG: NIGGAS!

DY: How do you even pronounce that? I tried to do it phonetically and my nose started bleeding.

PJ: Rah-kez is how he pronounced it

DY: I wish I knew a tenured sociologist here to explain the nigger named presidents phenomenon. I mean, it's obvious why there are so many black people with Washington and Jefferson as last names now. But what happened to all the white Washingtons and Jeffersons and Jacksons and Taylors and shit? Where they go?

PJ: They all changed their name; there were too many black Washingtons and Jeffersons

DY: That seems too obvious of an answer. That the same thing happened to Washington as a last name as Cadillac as a brand. What are you more likely to see—a white Washington or a white man whipping a coupe seville?

PJ: I wonder if all white areas are full of white Washingtons whippin' Cadillacs

DY: Like a multiverse whiteness?

SG: Exactly

Tenderheaded

✳

BRIAN BROOME

The kids in my neighborhood used to call them "kukkabubs" and my head was full of them. I stared them down every morning in the mirror, determined to vanquish them with a purple comb that was missing teeth. Teeth that had fallen in combat on the battleground that was my nappy-ass head. When I tried to comb my hair, I would hear those teeth break like guitar strings against the formidability of my kinks and fall to the bathroom floor. Then I would cry out in pain and my mother would shout through the bathroom door.

"What the hell you doing in there?"

It would have been less humiliating to shout "I'm just in here tryna massage my dick until it squirts!" than the actual truth. And the truth was that I was trying to get my hair to go as straight as I wished I was. And that the comb in my hand was no match for it. No more useful than my prayers every night that I would wake up heterosexual. But there I stood in that cursed mirror trying my best to eradicate both, my feet covered in broken comb teeth, my scalp aching, and my thoughts still drifting toward Michael Evans from *Good Times,* who is still the only man I've ever truly loved.

Don't nobody but me and the good Lord above know about the trials and tribulations that me and my hair have gone through. Because, when I was young, "nappy" was a bad word. Today, it's a celebration of naturalness, of pride, of beauty. But in the eighties, nappy hair was stigmatized. A sign of ugliness, shame, and, most of all, poverty. It was the era of the Jheri, S, and Classy Curl. The heyday of the hot comb, when Black hair sizzled like hot bacon grease. If you had nappy hair in the eighties, it was because your parents couldn't afford to buy the products necessary to make your hair as slick and shiny as a newborn baby. The conversations around "good hair" were long and frequent. The praise one would receive for having "good hair" was tantamount to the praise one might receive for going to war and coming back in one piece. As if you'd fought the Nappybeast and won and were rewarded with a head of hair that didn't break your comb, but invited it instead to run smoothly through your tresses without your ever uttering a sound that would cause your mother to think you might be in the bathroom masturbating.

The barbershop was the worst. Scobie's was our neighborhood place. The staff consisted of several young, handsome men who strutted around the shop talking about young, handsome, manly things. They had a masculine ease about them that I envied, wished I could imitate, and wanted, at the same time, to be close to. They all smelled like bergamot and talcum powder, and because they worked on one another, their haircuts were divine. Symmetrical as an M. C. Escher painting. Lines cut with precision made by a steady hand holding the sharpest of razors. They were beautiful.

Then, of course, there was Scobie himself. The old one.

Irascible and heavyset, Scobie was the shop's owner. Between his lips rested a chewed-up cigar. It sat there perpetually and bobbed up and down when he spoke, holding on for dear life for fear of what Scobie might do to it if it fell out. He was impatient and easily angered. His white smock was never pristinely white like the other barbers'. His was always stained with the thing he was eating. Usually streaked brown with meat grease or a barbecue sauce that was once red but had lingered so long it was losing its color. His nails were yellow from the cigars he smoked, and because of his lazy eye, the lenses on his glasses were thick enough to have been made by the government. They magnified his eyes to comic proportions. And, because of his poor eyesight, men would come into the shop and wait an interminably long time stacked on top of one another just so one of the younger barbers could tend to them, while Scobie's chair sat empty as my baseball glove. Yet he was the man my father chose for my first haircut and I remember it to this day.

On a chilly morning in the fall, my father brings me into the shop. I am ten years old. Before this, my mother managed my hair by simply shaving it all off. But the time has come for me to partake in this rite of passage. As I look around the shop, all the men there greet my father with extended handshakes and talk of work. The shop is dark inside despite the fact that it's sunny outside. There is a golden crucifix on the wall with white Jesus hanging off it. The shop smells like cigarettes and my uncle Jimmy's breath after he dips into his coat pocket to sip from his flask. The men all work at the steel mill, which, we didn't know then, would close in a few years, leaving all of them out of work and desperate. Turning some of them into not just weekend drunks but drunks of the quotidian variety. As I take in the shop, they all talk of sex with women and football. Things that don't interest me now and never will. Scobie is the ringleader. Of all the men there, he is the most masculine, putting the "grrr" in "gruff" and making loud proclamations that cause the perpetually unlit cigar he chews on to bounce dramatically, exposing the wet end inside his mouth. All other chairs are full. Scobie's is empty. My father introduces him to me and he shakes my hand too firmly, causing the knuckles to slide against each other painfully. He is perturbed by the weakness of my handshake and makes a disgusted face. And my wide-eyed fretful look causes his upper lip to curl over his cigar in an unmistakable snarl of disdain.

I have been cutting my own hair for a very long time now. No one else loves me enough to do it. Much like no one loves me enough to take a machete and cut their way through the Okavango. Because, just like the Okavango, my hair is tough terrain. Not to mention that should you accept the challenge of my nappiness, you will be subject to whining the likes of which you have never heard. My hair hurts.

So, for the past many years, when I see that what's on top of my head is starting to look unwieldy, I grab my trusty clippers and head to the bathroom, where I stare it down in the mirror, approaching my hair in the same way a farmer would a field before mowing. Emerging from my tidy clapboard house, I place my thumbs beneath the straps of my overalls and lean back on my heels as I survey the work to be done. I always start at the back even though I can't see it. Best to get it over with. I place the clippers at the nape of my neck and begin to mow it all down one strip at a time as I watch tangled coils of kukkabubs drop silently into the sink and onto the floor around me. I am careful. I make certain that I start shaving a new strip where the strip I've just shaved has ended. I take my time. And when I'm done, I take a good long look at myself in the mirror. Completely bald. My scalp is always a little ashy so I reach for the baby oil to shine it up. Then I take another long look, pleased with the results, and pat myself on the back for saving money. Later, I'll be told by someone, usually sitting behind me on the bus, that I've missed several spots at the back of my head.

But this idea that I'm saving money is just a lie that I tell myself. The real truth is that I have been afraid to go to a Black barbershop for decades. I have found that, as a gay man, I just do not fit in there. Black barbershops are places where Black men bond over the kinds of things that heterosexual men bond over. Sporting events and sports figures that I have never heard of. They talk about women in ways that I have never experienced. In my younger years, I found the environment to be oppressively masculine. And, as a result, felt threatened and unwelcome. For me, the Black barbershop has been a place to endure pain. All kinds of pain.

After my father and Scobie catch up, Scobie leads me toward his chair, which may as well have cobwebs on it. The green vinyl that covers it is cracked in places where untold patrons must have sat in it long ago when he had good eyes. He starts by flinging a cloth that used to be white over my head. It lands softly around my shoulders and smells like Tide, the laundry soap my mother uses. He affixes a tissue paper collar around my neck and ties the piece of cloth too tightly around it.

"Cain't be too careful with these young'ns," he says to my father. "They like to squirm."

I hear the clippers roar to life behind me like the engine of a dirt bike and I feel the hair at the back of my neck stand on end. Scobie is not gentle. He dives into my naps with all the delicacy of a lumberjack determined to fell an oak. He pushes the clippers into my skull, in an effort, I guess, to make sure he only has to do one pass over that area, singularly focused on getting to the root of my problem. At first, I hold back the tears because I can see my father sitting in a chair across from me watching my every move. The other men in the shop are still engaged in their various conversations about Kareem Abdul Mohammed and Muhammad Ali and the Honorable Elijah Muhammad because all sports stars at this time have some version of "Muhammad" in their name. All the while, Scobie is going after my scalp like it has somehow wronged him, like he hates it. It seems to me that he is doing this on purpose. Something in the ugly look he gave me when he shook my limp hand makes me feel like he's doing this on purpose. I cast my eyes upward to white Jesus on the wall and silently pray to him for help. He ignores me because he's dealing with his own shit right now. I feel tufts of hair loosen and fall gently dead against my ears, screaming in pain on the way down. Scobie's clippers have to have blood on them. I just know that they have to have blood on them from my scalp.

He is catching nap after painful nap, and with each whimper I emit, he goes in harder, until I can't take it anymore and the tears start to flow. They flow freely and he announces as if to the entire barbershop . . .

"Whatchu cryin' 'bout?"

All the men turn and look. It's like he was waiting for this moment. He asks the question again and I don't answer. He keeps cutting. He is nowhere near finished. He decides to out me to the shop again.

"Boy, quit cryin'. Ain't nobody doin' nothin' to you."

The look on my father's face is embarrassment mixed with a simmering anger. His humiliation is total as he stands to walk toward me. As he approaches, I can feel the heat of his emotions. He bends down to whisper in my ear.

"Stop all that cryin', now," he says, and presses the blade farther into my scalp.

So I suck it up. I choke back the remainder of the tears and only wince occasionally. I suffer through until the last of the hair falls to the floor and Scobie whips the backward cape off me as if he's a magician who's just performed a trick. And what a trick it was. I look in the mirror.

Scobie's failing eyes have completely abandoned the idea of symmetry. My head looks like God was distracted when he put it on. The cut somehow makes my eyes look uneven and my ears detachable, like I'm a Mr. Potato Head. My father actually pays this man for the torture and the botched haircut. He even tips him. In the car on the way home, he and I sit in silence.

It's not the physical pain of that experience that has kept me away from the barbershop. Physical pain is often fleeting. What kept me away was the energy of these spaces. Tinged with hypermasculine musk, shows of dominance and submission, and, of course, homophobia. I have sat in countless barber chairs listening to the men around me crack jokes about "punks" and "fags." I would listen silently as the clippers buzzed around my ears. And, one day, I just decided to stop going and to give myself awful haircuts. The embarrassment of having the patch of hair at the back of my head laughed at was nowhere near the anxiety and embarrassment I felt from having to enter and linger in a space that was clearly not meant for me.

Anxiety is a bitch. I have lived with it all my life. I live with the kind of anxiety that doesn't just keep me confined to my neighborhood, or my house. I have the kind of anxiety that can, when it wants to, keep me confined to my room. A single room all day long. And, this year, I decided that I'd had enough. So, I moved from the cold and gray clutches of Appalachia to sunny California. The culture shock was overwhelming.

And I decided that, as long as I was tossing things aside that didn't serve me, I would also overcome my fear of the Black barbershop.

After a couple of months of California life, I looked in the mirror and saw that my hair was growing longer in some places and not growing at all in others. Patchy and erratic. I had walked by my neighborhood barbershop several times every day. Through the window was an old man. I could tell just by looking at him that this shop was his. He sat in one of his own barber chairs and never looked up from his newspaper. And, one day, I decided to go in.

When I walked through the door, the bell just over my head rang, alerting him to my presence, and that's pretty much all it did. It alerted him. And the only reason I know that is because his eyes briefly looked up from his newspaper. He didn't say shit. Didn't move shit. Didn't feel shit. I stood there awkwardly for a full minute before he spoke.

"Well, sit down if you gonna sit down."

I sat down.

I have never seen something so old move without benefit of pall-bearers. He was slow, creaky, and fueled by evil. I wondered if I should maybe ask him if he needed help but then thought better of it. Something told me that offering help to this man would be tantamount to offering to fuck his wife. And I didn't want that smoke.

When he finally got behind me, he put on a sparkling white barber coat, covered me in a fresh linen, put that weird tape around my neck, and spoke.

"Whatchu want?"

"Can you just cut it low?"

Methuselah went to work. He spoke, but I couldn't tell if he was speaking to me or not.

"Damn Republicans."

"What?"

Then nothing. He'd clam right up. It was like I didn't need to be there at all. When he finally addressed me directly . . .

"Yo head crooked."

"Excuse me?"

"You got a crooked-ass head. I gotta practically stand on one foot to get it lined up."

"Nobody ever told me that before."

"Well . . . they shudda. And you got a big dent in the middla yo head."

"Interesting story there," I said. "When I was a kid—"

"Shhh."

He cut my hair in silence. Cut it perfectly. Lines straight as an architect's. Shading impeccable. He handed me a mirror, again without a word. I had to compliment him.

"Good job."

"I know."

I gave him his money and a generous tip. He shoved it into his jacket pocket without looking at it. Then he told me . . .

"You go on out there and look good for a change."

I left his shop feeling more free. But I also knew that he and I could never be friends. I could tell by the religious signs on his wall, one of which proudly exclaimed that his guns and his faith were the most important things to him. I could tell by his silence that he had adopted the masculine pose of stoicism and gruffness. Just like Scobie. I could tell that, if he knew I was gay, he might just ask me to leave and never come back. But my real problem with him was none of these things. My real problem is that I have always felt like it is my job to fit in, to be accepted. I realized that I have always lusted to be "one of the boys" even though I clearly am not. My real problem is a discomfort with myself that includes wanting to gain the approval of people who, quite frankly, don't care if I live or die.

That night, after my haircut, I went on a date with a nice man. We sat over dinner at a fancy Oakland restaurant and talked about all the minutiae that one talks about on dates. I told him about my job, my family, my cat. He did the same. But during a lull in the conversation, his eyes fixed on my head just above my eyes and he announced, "Your haircut is fly." He asked me where I got it done and I told him. Later on, I pointed out the shop as he drove me back to my place, came inside, and spent the night. All thoughts of Scobie and haircuts and needing to belong miraculously disappeared. I went back to my California barber only once more. And when he said something about "punks," I started cutting my own hair again.

But, as time wore on, I decided to give someone else another try. I looked up a barber near me and just went for it. I walked through the door with all the trepidation I held for barbershops clinging to me. But this time wasn't like the others. As I took a seat with all the other men doing and talking about all the manly things that have always been beyond my reach, I broke out into a cold sweat.

My current barber is young. And apart from holding conversations with the other young man who cuts hair with him and laughing at patrons' jokes, he is mostly silent. But he is friendly and greets me warmly when I come in. And he gives a good haircut, which, for me, is easy. Now that I am older, my thinning hair only calls for one prescription. Shave it down close. Try to make my crooked head look less crooked.

I wrote a book about my experiences as a Black, gay man in a world where too many people still think that those two things together don't make sense. The book did well and I'm proud of it.

As I sit in my new barber's chair about to get my monthly shave, a young man walks in and we lock eyes. I see a look of recognition in his that, at first, makes me worry. But then he smiles. He asks me my name and I tell him.

"Aww, man," he says. "I read your book!"

He then proceeds to announce to everyone in the barbershop that he read my book and that it was "dope." I have received no higher compliment. Then he disappears out the door, leaving me to explain to my new barber what the book is about. He tells me enthusiastically that "that's what up" and the rest of the men in the shop praise me as well. The young man who recognized me then comes charging through the door. Breathless. He is holding a copy of the book that he's just purchased from the bookstore up the street and asks me to sign it right then and there. Of course I do. But to my surprise, he asks me to make it out to the barbershop in which I am currently sitting. And so I do. I make it out to the Natural Choice barbershop and I think I write something thanking them for always giving me good haircuts. The barbers place the book proudly on a shelf where everyone who gets a haircut can see it. And here is where this story should naturally come to an end. When the protagonist has come full circle. When all he has been through comes to a tidy end. An end so clean and precise that its lines are almost architectural. Where the errant hairs are dusted off and fall to the floor. And where the protagonist is spun around to look in a mirror and can say nothing more than "That's perfect."

How to Shit in West Virginia at Night: But for Niggas?

KIESE LAYMON

From: Damon Young <dame&young@gmail.com>
To: Kiese Laymon <keeeznuts@gmail.com>
Subject: black humor and shit

Fam, you still down to be a part of this anthology? The streets are talking.

From: Kiese Laymon <keeeznuts@gmail.com>
To: Damon Young <dame&young@gmail.com>
Re: Subject: black humor and shit

Absolutely! When is it due?

From: Damon Young <dame&young@gmail.com>
To: Kiese Laymon <keeeznuts@gmail.com>
Re: Subject: black humor and shit

August 1st sound good? Also what do you want to write? (Also also, your tweet about Trump's high and juicy booty is my guiding light for this anthology. Might even try to get it in there somehow.)

From: Kiese Laymon <keeeznuts@gmail.com>
To: Damon Young <dame&young@gmail.com>
Re: Subject: black humor and shit

> That sounds good. Definitely use the tweet. I was gonna write a "how to" on public toilets use for niggas 47, fat and tired.

From: Damon Young <dame&young@gmail.com>
To: Kiese Laymon <keeeznuts@gmail.com>
Re: Subject: black humor and shit

> Say more. Related, me and Brentin Mock actually have a running list of which public bathrooms to use in which neighborhoods in Pittsburgh—a helpful guide for middle-aged niggas with sensitive stomachs.

From: Kiese Laymon <keeeznuts@gmail.com>
To: Damon Young <dame&young@gmail.com>
Re: Subject: black humor and shit

> Sensitive-stomach-ass niggas. So I think I wanna write a "how-to" piece on public toilets and I think I'll center the piece on that drive from New York to Mississippi. It's mostly I-81, which is a monster, because if you don't watch out, you'll be shitting in a urinal in West Virginia where ain't nothing black in the whole town except dookie on the mirror.

From: Damon Young <dame&young@gmail.com>
To: Kiese Laymon <keeeznuts@gmail.com>
Re: Subject: black humor and shit

> You shitted in a urinal in West Virginia?

From: Kiese Laymon <keeeznuts@gmail.com>
To: Damon Young <dame&young@gmail.com>
Re: Subject: black humor and shit

Nah, it wasn't like that.

From: Damon Young <dame&young@gmail.com>
To: Kiese Laymon <keeeznuts@gmail.com>
Re: Subject: black humor and shit

You shitted in West Virginia? How was that?

From: Kiese Laymon <keeeznuts@gmail.com>
To: Damon Young <dame&young@gmail.com>
Re: Subject: black humor and shit

That's what I want to write about. It involves more than six T-shirts, some wet wipes, and Funyuns. Thinking about titles already.
   "How to Shit in West Virginia"

From: Damon Young <dame&young@gmail.com>
To: Kiese Laymon <keeeznuts@gmail.com>
Re: Subject: black humor and shit

Too HBO.

From: Kiese Laymon <keeeznuts@gmail.com>
To: Damon Young <dame&young@gmail.com>
Re: Subject: black humor and shit

   "How to Shit in West Virginia at Night"

From: Damon Young <dame&young@gmail.com>
To: Kiese Laymon <keeeznuts@gmail.com>
Re: Subject: black humor and shit

A little too F/X. You see what Kyrie just posted on IG? wonder if he'll contribute to the anthology.

From: Kiese Laymon <keeeznuts@gmail.com>
To: Damon Young <dame&young@gmail.com>
Re: Subject: black humor and shit

I ain't see it. But he remind me of Lamont Sanford.
   "How to Shit in West Virginia at Night: But for Niggas?"

From: Damon Young <dame&young@gmail.com>
To: Kiese Laymon <keeeznuts@gmail.com>
Re: Subject: black humor and shit

Perfect. BET+ perfection.

From: Kiese Laymon <keeeznuts@gmail.com>
To: Damon Young <dame&young@gmail.com>
Re: Subject: black humor and shit

Okay, so I can turn that in probably next week. But here's what I was telling you about. So you know how we see you as the Black Yoda of Therapy?
   Yoda Black.

From: Damon Young <dame&young@gmail.com>
To: Kiese Laymon <keeeznuts@gmail.com>
Re: Subject: black humor and shit

Why are you emailing me this?

From: Kiese Laymon <keeeznuts@gmail.com>
To: Damon Young <dame&young@gmail.com>
Re: Subject: black humor and shit

Yoda Black, have you ever hated a nigga who could squat?

From: Damon Young <dame&young@gmail.com>
To: Kiese Laymon <keeeznuts@gmail.com>
Re: Subject: black humor and shit

What does that mean? Like in the weight room?

From: Kiese Laymon <keeeznuts@gmail.com>
To: Damon Young <dame&young@gmail.com>
Re: Subject: black humor and shit

I mean, kinda. Sure. Definitely. But also any kind of squat. I hate
niggas who can squat down.

From: Damon Young <dame&young@gmail.com>
To: Kiese Laymon <keeeznuts@gmail.com>
Re: Subject: black humor and shit

You hate like 98% of niggas under 65?

From: Kiese Laymon <keeeznuts@gmail.com>
To: Damon Young <dame&young@gmail.com>
Re: Subject: black humor and shit

That's what I'm saying. Is it anti-black to hate niggas who can squat
down. A nigga was delivering my mail today and he dropped a little
Best Buy coupon right in front of both of us. This arthritis in my hips
just wouldn't let me even fake I could pick it up. But this mailman-ass
nigga squatted so fucking deep to pick up that coupon bruh.
    I don't know if I ever hated a nigga more in my entire life.

From: Damon Young <dame&young@gmail.com>
To: Kiese Laymon <keeeznuts@gmail.com>
Re: Subject: black humor and shit

Why are you emailing me this? Do you hate white boys who can squat?

From: Kiese Laymon <keeeznuts@gmail.com>
To: Damon Young <dame&young@gmail.com>
Re: Subject: black humor and shit

Yes. But not as much. Hardly at all. Plus they don't squat right. It's a way to squat if you have thighs like most niggas. And they squat the opposite of that. They bend deeply. Niggas with thighs and ass be squatting.

From: Damon Young <dame&young@gmail.com>
To: Kiese Laymon <keeeznuts@gmail.com>
Re: Subject: black humor and shit

Don't ever have this conversation with anyone else. Do you hate black women who can squat?

From: Kiese Laymon <keeeznuts@gmail.com>
To: Damon Young <dame&young@gmail.com>
Re: Subject: black humor and shit

I do not. I'm rather thankful.

From: Damon Young <dame&young@gmail.com>
To: Kiese Laymon <keeeznuts@gmail.com>
Re: Subject: black humor and shit

Do you hate white women who can squat?

From: Kiese Laymon <keeeznuts@gmail.com>
To: Damon Young <dame&young@gmail.com>
Re: Subject: black humor and shit

I want to say I do. But I do not.

From: Damon Young <dame&young@gmail.com>
To: Kiese Laymon <keeeznuts@gmail.com>
Re: Subject: black humor and shit

I think I understand now. You shitted in a urinal in West Virginia, not because the toilet was gross but because you have arthritis in your hips and you can no longer squat like most niggas. So, instead of hating arthritis or hating the white shitters who fucked up the toilet, or instead of using the insurance the white people at your job give you to get that fixed, you want to hate niggas who can squat?

From: Kiese Laymon <keeeznuts@gmail.com>
To: Damon Young <dame&young@gmail.com>
Re: Subject: black humor and shit

I mean, that's not my story but if I knew more about that story from a nigga like the nigga you talking about, would you want that in your anthology?

From: Damon Young <dame&young@gmail.com>
To: Kiese Laymon <keeeznuts@gmail.com>
Re: Subject: black humor and shit

Absolutely.

From: Damon Young <dame&young@gmail.com>
To: Kiese Laymon <keeeznuts@gmail.com>
Re: Subject: black humor and shit

So I got a confession.

From: Kiese Laymon <keeeznuts@gmail.com>
To: Damon Young <dame&young@gmail.com>
Re: Subject: black humor and shit

My nigga.

From: Kiese Laymon <keeeznuts@gmail.com>
To: Damon Young <dame&young@gmail.com>
Re: Subject: black humor and shit

What's that?

From: Damon Young <dame&young@gmail.com>
To: Kiese Laymon <keeeznuts@gmail.com>
Re: Subject: black humor and shit

You ever see *Dune*?

From: Kiese Laymon <keeeznuts@gmail.com>
To: Damon Young <dame&young@gmail.com>
Re: Subject: black humor and shit

The movie where Timothee Chalamet is white Jesus?

From: Damon Young <dame&young@gmail.com>
To: Kiese Laymon <keeeznuts@gmail.com>
Re: Subject: black humor and shit

Yup.

From: Kiese Laymon <keeeznuts@gmail.com>
To: Damon Young <dame&young@gmail.com>
Re: Subject: black humor and shit

Why?

From: Damon Young <dame&young@gmail.com>
To: Kiese Laymon <keeeznuts@gmail.com>
Re: Subject: black humor and shit

So remember at the end of the movie, when White Jesus and his mama get through the desert and escape that brolic-ass sand worm, and then they run into all them Nike Huarache–ass niggas and Zendaya?

From: Kiese Laymon <keeeznuts@gmail.com>
To: Damon Young <dame&young@gmail.com>
Re: Subject: black humor and shit

Yup.

From: Damon Young <dame&young@gmail.com>
To: Kiese Laymon <keeeznuts@gmail.com>
Re: Subject: black humor and shit

I feel like Zendaya looks like how everyone 30 years ago said everyone was gonna look like in 2020. But I was alive in 1990, and everyone looks the same as they did then.

From: Kiese Laymon <keeeznuts@gmail.com>
To: Damon Young <dame&young@gmail.com>
Re: Subject: black humor and shit

She look like the sister of every NBA lottery pick last year.

From: Damon Young <dame&young@gmail.com>
To: Kiese Laymon <keeeznuts@gmail.com>
Re: Subject: black humor and shit

> She do look like her little brother ball for the Warriors. Is it racist to
> say that?

From: Kiese Laymon <keeeznuts@gmail.com>
To: Damon Young <dame&young@gmail.com>
Re: Subject: black humor and shit

> Probably. But niggas can't be racist. Black people can though.

From: Damon Young <dame&young@gmail.com>
To: Kiese Laymon <keeeznuts@gmail.com>
Re: Subject: black humor and shit

> True facts. But yeah, so when White Jesus meets the Huarache
> niggas, the darkest-skinned one (because racism) challenges him
> to a duel. Not sure exactly why. Maybe just for the honor of taking
> Zendaya to the Huarache nigga prom. And while Huarache Nigga Pat
> Bev is waiting for White Jesus to prepare for the fight, this nigga just
> sits in a full squat for like 17 minutes straight. It's the most impressive
> thing I've ever seen. I've also never hated a man more. So anyway,
> I too hate niggas who can squat.

From: Kiese Laymon <keeeznuts@gmail.com>
To: Damon Young <dame&young@gmail.com>
Re: Subject: black humor and shit

> My nigga.

Drive Me Crazy

✳

SHAMIRA IBRAHIM

When you are a child, it takes you a while to realize that parents, like any other human on earth, lie. They will lie to get you to take your medicine; lie to convince you to shut up and do your homework; to get you to simply stop asking for something over and over again. These are fairly innocuous lies of convenience, but there are also lies born out of irritation: once, my mom spent an entire evening insisting that my brother was adopted and would be sent back just because he didn't rinse dishes.

My mom's tall tales were generally impulsive and petty, largely born out of exhaustion in trying to reconcile the strict East African Muslim upbringing she knew with her children's rambunctious adventures in Harlem. Her go-to was negotiating TV time for my favorite shows in exchange for me studying the Quran for an hour without complaint. Only problem was, our TV was rarely connected to standard broadcast, much less cable; she would have to resort to borrowing bootleg movies to placate her kids.

My father, on the other hand, always had a flair for the dramatic. Day in and day out, without fail, he would take his morning trip downtown, the latest copy of the *Wall Street Journal* rolled into his right hand. His uniform was consistent: a faux-leather briefcase and classic gray trench in his best imitation of a nineties Black conservative sitcom dad with business affairs to tend to. He would regularly regale me with his endeavors and dreams—I still remember the car he always intended on buying, a silver BMW 530i. He recounted to me his lunch meetings at Windows on the World, the trendy restaurant du jour atop the Twin Towers. He sold me the fantasy of the enterprising businessman—one who spelled "honor" with the British U and consistently mingled with high-flyers in finance. It was an illusion that I wanted to believe, even if we had to keep our cereal in the fridge so that roaches wouldn't get in.

My dad was effortlessly charming and so committed to his self-mythology that I simply could not help but believe him. As far as I was concerned, he was the Philip Banks of the projects—if Philip Banks's suitcase was regularly filled with stolen AOL dial-up internet free trial CDs from post offices throughout Harlem. Once, he woke me to sit in front of our gargantuan Compaq Presario and write out some business plans, a routine that would become standard for that summer. He would open his worn composition notebook and dictate to me, in English and French, his grand plan for what he called the "African Sky Project": a grand initiative to revolutionize the telecoms on the East African coast by positioning satellites along the Swahili region. I sat in my nightgown every weekend and transcribed his dreams as he worked to send his ambitious business plans from his Hotmail account to the investment departments at JPMorgan Chase, Bear Stearns, and the United Nations project teams. I had no concept of how outlandish his plans were—an unemployed undocumented immigrant asking for hundreds of millions in financing when my parents could barely afford to let me get snacks from the corner store after school. But this was simply my weekly ritual. Business with Dad and then a few episodes of *Arthur*. Which I'd miss more often than not, because his lessons would run long. To make it up to me, he'd let me eat a frozen or prepackaged food item Mom wouldn't let me have—a terrible compromise, as my dad regularly attempted to feed me and my brother Kraft mac and cheese without the powdered cheese. (No one eats just the Kraft mac.)

And then 9/11 happened. Which, for a family full of Black Muslims with Arabic names, was like . . . being a family full of Black Muslims with Arabic names in America after 9/11. But I largely remember that day as the one when I began to realize just how much of a liar my own father was. I was sitting in middle school in Harlem as parents began to call their kids, and a classmate rushed into the room screaming, "The Twin Towers fell!" We laughed at first. Who could believe something so outlandish? But as the truth sank in, I began to panic. *That's where Dad works.* On the bus home, I was overcome by dread. *That's where Dad works.*

I confronted my mom with tears in my eyes. *Is Dad okay?* She laughed like she was explaining a riddle I wasn't old enough to solve and told me he was nowhere near there. I wasn't in on the joke yet, so I was equal parts relieved and confused. *We're never going to eat at Windows on the World after all.* When he finally strolled home, hours later, he told us that God saved him by stopping the train before it got to Chambers Street—which I later learned was a common lie from New Yorkers with terrorism FOMO.

My high school years brought the farce into full focus. Suddenly, my father was asking to borrow my student MetroCard to go to work conferences at the Javits Center. *What businessman doesn't have $3 for a trip back and forth from downtown?* My parents would fight, loud enough that the cops occasionally came to the door. The first time the police told him to leave was the first time I discovered that my beloved entrepreneur and financial savant was not only not on the lease but not even legally married to my mom. I opened the envelope to the overdue bill for the cable, which had long since been disconnected, hoping to understand why I didn't have access to *Taina* on Nickelodeon anymore, only to not see my dad's or mom's name on the bill, but that of a family friend who had long since stopped coming by to visit (I later found out my dad ruined his credit). Was dad . . . *a scammer?* Growing up in Harlem, I was familiar with a hustle, but I had never considered that we were the marks.

The thing about lifelong trauma is that it completely warps your perception of what is supposed to be "normal." Normal is an elusive social contract that you only become accustomed to via trial by fire— say or do the wrong thing at the wrong time in enough instances and you quickly get a gauge of what is and isn't acceptable in polite society. There are the small hiccups, like the first time in elementary school I proudly said that my dad was an "entrepreneur"—I wouldn't learn until high school that it was effectively synonymous with "unemployed." Then there were the bigger missteps, such as the time I told my program advisors that my dad worked in "international business," prompting an investigation against my mom over whether we truly lived in the projects. The hijinks slowly started to challenge everything I thought was real—the phone calls I got from the Nintendo store and Toys "R" Us because my dad thought that leaving my brother at a toy store substituted for using a babysitting service while he went to spread his business cards at the Javits Center; the flip phone I was gifted my senior year of high school that was cut off in less than a week because it had been activated fraudulently. I was my dad's cover story, and was none the wiser until I started to brag to friends who asked follow-up questions I had no answers to. How could my dad go on a business trip to Switzerland when we were all undocumented? *That nigga was probably cheating,* my best friend guessed (and she was right—there was a white lady in Long Island who stayed blowing our house phone up).

I was humiliated and embarrassed, but I mainly became resentful. The image of my dazzlingly intelligent six-feet-two father who charmed everyone around him was flattened by the villain who embarrassed me. He was now the man who wore the same ratty three-piece suit every day, lingering in the lobby like a troll as he waited for me to get home from school to let him in after Mom changed the locks on him. When he would walk me to the train, the language had shifted from big business dreams to venomous rambles on how evil Mom was and how she was trying to keep him from me. He even began to pop up at my school during big events, mingling with other adults whose parents *were* legit businessmen and doctors and lawyers while charming them with his grand ideas. I would sit nearby in my worn-out all-white Air Force 1s, desperately hoping to disappear. The more chaotic my home life became, the bigger of a show he made, and he began to look like shit too.

Once I went to college, I cut ties with him. I couldn't take the turmoil and the lies anymore, and I only wanted to communicate with my parents on an as-needed basis. Who can Dutty Wine after a voicemail from a deranged dad? My sophomore year, I learned he had been caught in the daily blotter, and I concealed my shame as I read the report during Econ 201: *"A credit-card thief was grabbed by police after he was caught lurking inside a posh East Side hotel, authorities said yesterday . . . Cops approached Ibrahim and found stolen items in his possession, including credit and debit cards, a wallet and a cell phone, investigators said."*

So my dad is a scammer, I thought to myself as I gulped whatever cocktail of jungle juice was available that night. I regaled my friends with what I then believed were funny stories of Dad the scammer, and woke to a glorious hangover. I even almost convinced myself I'd been the life of the party and not the nigga vomiting out trauma while everyone stared in uncomfortable awe.

For several years, this method of compartmentalization worked. Then came the emails.

Sent: Sun, Apr 17 3:59 pm
Subject: Fwd:

I hope you celebrated Shamira's 25th birthday with joy. It worths to remind you that both of you conspired to get me arrested and put me on jail for the wrong reason. That the worst conspiracy I ever heard from a mom and her daughter.

You both wish I'M DEAD by now since YOU, Fatima, tried again to make up another false story to the Police to sent me on prison for the rest of my life. Well! I'm sorry that this time they didn't believe you but, at least you have realized your AMERICAN DREAM by kick me out of the house, prevent me to raise my children and bring those bastards in your bed. It was those deeds, among many others which make you the Sadistic Woman. What a shame! You may have escaped but, trust me, soon or later, justice will be served.

I had been accused of many things—precociousness, self-righteousness, obnoxiousness, long-windedness, know-it-all syndrome, and just general discontent and inability to read the room—but a grand conspiracy to get my father arrested and deported was a new one.

The emails came fast and furious, each more delusional than the last. Supporting characters included drug dealers, criminals, Jews, the American court system, false police reports, the significance of Thanksgiving, my brother's Facebook account, the World Bank. Each email dumbfounded me in its absurdity, conviction, and deteriorating grammar. The man I knew was a stickler for performing poshness, yet these were the accusations of a raving madman.

The emails have continued for years. In 2023, he introduced a new clown in his circus: Donald Trump.

Sent: Thurs, March 30 9:25 pm
Subject: Law vs Hate

The indictment of their Former President, Donald Trump, brought old memories. I happen to know the guy before he run for the White House. Tone sure, I am in his mailing list and met almost everyone from his family.

Without being said, I have no connection with him and never ever being fun of his ideology, quite the opposite. I'm bringing this up today for reason. If Donald Trump ended by going to jail, that will be because a grand jury convicted him.

My case is very different. I am probably the ONLY PERSON on earth who was put on jail by a Sadistic person who make fake story in order to be with her Drug Dealers. Her wish was that I will ended by dying in custody. She just forgot one thing, THERE IS JUSTICE ON EARTH.

At this point, I hadn't seen my dad in person in over fifteen years. I shared these emails with my therapist. She was stone silent. This couldn't possibly be the charming schemer whom I constantly and begrudgingly praised for giving me my intellect; he barely knew how to properly execute subject-verb agreement, and didn't always seem to have the best grasp of what day it was. The closest comparative I could give to her was how I recognized the trauma that I felt in Kanye West's family—struggling to reconcile the genius they knew him to be with the deranged conspiratorialist he had now become. The main difference between my dad and Kanye, aside from the incomprehensible wealth, shuttered sunglasses, and sterile mansions, of course, is that I don't for a second believe my father has met or spent time with the Trump family outside of loitering in front of their many eponymously named towers throughout Manhattan.

Despite this tangible evidence, I was still stunned at the assessment my therapist gave me. "I haven't spent time with him personally to formally diagnose him, but based on everything you've told me, I think there's a strong possibility that your father has been living with an untreated personality disorder." *Dad, crazy? Not the man who taught me how to read and went through business plans with me.* It took quite a long time to reframe the reality of my childhood memories through the lens of mental illness—his "business plans" as manic ideas, his frayed three-piece suits as feeding his delusions, and his financial fiascos as consequences of his lack of impulse control. It was hard, but it was necessary. The only thing I dreaded was finally bringing it to my mom, the woman who once told me that "we all get sad sometimes" as a reaction to my being diagnosed with clinical depression.

After a few weeks of processing, I steeled myself to discuss this possibility with her over lunch. "Oh," she said, unfazed. "I see how that can make sense. The last time your dad was arrested, they asked me if he had bipolar disorder and needed to be checked out. I knew nothing about that so I said no, but I guess they were right."

I sat silent for several seconds and then burst into heaving laughter at the realization that Mom had known all along. Crazy or not, my parents are impeccable liars.

We Don't Make Princesses in Those Colors

NICOLA YOON

During the first couple of months of my little girl's life, my primary goal was ensuring she didn't die on my watch. I forgot about the accepted standards of personal hygiene and fashion. What I could not forget about was my daughter, not even for a single second of every minute of every day. The entire world had suddenly transformed itself into a vast spiky pit of nonstop peril. Choking hazards included: All toys, all foods, my daughter's own fingers and toes. The fingers and toes of my husband. The fingers and toes of . . . me. And the things that weren't trying to choke her were trying to maim her. She was like a divining rod, discovering danger at every turn. No amount of child-proofing could prevent her unerring ability to find a sharp corner designed expressly to puncture the fontanelles on her skull. Most days I imagined myself to be a goalkeeper, deflecting shot after shot during a never-ending overtime shoot-out from hell.

Time passed. My daughter became a toddler, and then a preschooler. The myriad swirling threats shifted their tactics away from her physical safety and trained their pentagram-shaped reticles onto her emotional and spiritual soft spots—the fontanelles, as it were—of her still-developing soul.

I put away my goalie uniform, changed into cleric's robes instead, and gave her what I hoped was wisdom. I encouraged her to be kind, brave, and curious. I taught her to always do the extra credit and that mushrooms are a perfect food.

But what I really wanted most of all was for her to love *herself*. Part of loving yourself is loving the skin you're in. I mean this not just metaphorically but quite literally. I needed to teach her how to love her brown skin. But how to pull this off in a country with as big of a race problem as America? America, a country that loves the *idea* that all men are created equal, but not the practice? How was I going to teach her that she was smart and beautiful and could be anyone she wanted to be when the entire country and its media minions told her otherwise? Or worse, erased her outright? How many cartoons and TV shows to this day still insist on featuring only white boys and girls, as if almost all people of color have been bred out of existence by some clandestine eugenics conspiracy? And of the few characters who have managed to dodge the (hypothetical) sterilization needle, how many are relegated to the position of lowly sidekick?

This struggle to show my little girl positive representation is something I work at every day. I expose her to media that depicts characters of color in an honest way. I teach her our history.

But what else can I be doing? It's a question I'm always asking myself. It's a question that presented itself at a pizza party six years ago when she was just five years old.

Now, if you have small children of your own, you know that pizza is eaten at every kid's birthday party, and there is a kid's birthday party—and I am not kidding about this—five times every weekend. My body became pizza-shaped during those days. So did my husband's face.

Anyway. The one I'm about to tell you about was held at a local pizza place, where the kids made their *own* pies. Picture twenty five-year-olds and their parents kneading dough, spreading sauce, sprinkling cheese, and layering pepperoni. By the way, for a kid's party, there is no other topping on earth or in Eden aside from pepperoni. Like most everything involving five-year-olds, pizza-making was complete chaos and, actually, pretty fun too. One girl topped her pizza with so much cheese and pepperoni that the resulting pie was six inches high. Think about that.

While the "pizzas" were baking, the kids lined up to get balloons made. I'm pretty certain this is still standard fare for a five-year-old's party, although these days who knows, maybe kids line up to get custom NFTs or therapist time with an AI-powered clown.

I'm not here to speculate about any of that. At this particular party there was a balloon artist and she was *good*. Beyond good. She was *virtuosic*. She could make anything the kids asked of her, and she was *fast*. The kids didn't even have time to get impatient and whiny. They were too enthralled. The woman was a master, whipping and twisting and squeaking out elaborate creations with full-on no-look dexterity. She made foot-long flower crowns, castles, even a car. I wanted her to re-create my early thirties but waited for the children to go first.

After pizza and juice, the balloon woman decided to make more masterpieces to leave behind—extras in case some child inevitably popped their own by a frustratingly preventable "accident," like sticking a pencil into it. By making backups, she was graciously sparing us poor parents future tears and drama. A professional through and through. Among her standard swords, butterflies, and crowns, what most impressed me were her elaborate princesses: complete with hair and arms and a gown. She drew a face on each with a black marker. I'd never seen anything like it. But my amazement was short-lived.

All the princesses were white.

Which is to say, the balloon woman had used the peach balloons blown up into perfect spheres for the faces. I noticed this after the fifth or sixth balloon pirouetted by. With growing incredulity, I peered at the balloon arsenal on the woman's tool belt. There were three shades of brown balloons: Thandiwe, Serena, and Lupita. Okay. My little girl was too busy eating cake in a fugue state using both fists to notice the princesses, but eventually maybe she'd want one, and I wanted to give her one in her skin color. I would hand it to her, a wordlessly no-big-deal but actually profound life lesson that, look, brown princess balloons existed. *My daughter* existed.

I went over to the balloon woman—nay, artiste—and asked her if she could make one using one of the brown balloons for the face. She replied (and I'm quoting, because I can never forget, no matter how I try, her exact words) with this:

"We don't make princesses in those colors."

I blurted out that I didn't understand. The requisite balloons were right there on her tool belt. She said yes, she had brown balloons, but they weren't the right type—something about their elasticity—to make faces. Then she went back to maniacally making her peach princess with a shrug. A *shrug*.

I was so taken aback that I didn't know what to say. I might have nodded and wandered off bleating like a concussed goat. I found my husband. I told him about the exchange. I won't repeat what he said (*Fucking racist balloon bitch!*) but he was angry.

Now, I'm a nonconfrontational person. Fights make me uncomfortable. I avoid them if I can. Moreover, I'm a sunny sort. Optimistic. A benefit-of-the-doubt giver, and a grateful benefit-of-the-doubt beneficiary. I believe that people are mostly good. I believe that if people know the right thing to do, they'll mostly do it.

So, like the sunny sort that I am, I believed her about the brown balloons. I had no reason not to. I'm a writer, not a balloon-maker. Maybe the brown ones really weren't the right type for making faces. Maybe their particular dye requires them to be specced to some other . . . PSI . . . inflation . . . tolerance quotient . . . thing. I don't think the balloon woman lied to me because she didn't *want* to make a brown princess. What I found astonishing was that she'd never *thought* to make brown faces in the first place.

Surely, I couldn't have been the first person to ask. Why hadn't it mattered to her to get the proper brown balloons?

My husband asked me if I wanted him to say something (other than what he'd said at first). I said no. I wanted to do it.

I went back over to her and I said: "It's not okay that you don't make princesses in that color." She started to explain again about the types of balloons. I was polite. I was and still am not a balloon expert. I heard her out.

Then I said: "It's still not okay. There are brown princesses. There are Black princesses and it's not okay for you to do that."

We made eye contact and I held it. She nodded and said, "Okay." And I walked away again.

I don't know if what I said mattered to her. I don't know if she ever went out and got brown balloons with the correct elasticity, or if she simply carried on making peach princesses at every party thereafter. I wish I could end this essay by saying that I went home and promptly learned how to make brown balloon princesses, but I did not. Who's got time for all that?

In the end my little girl was too busy eating cake to even notice the princesses. Besides, she was happy with her sword, which lasted another two days before it deflated.

These days, I think I'm doing okay protecting my little girl's fontanelles. She loves writing stories and illustrating them. As it turns out, she doesn't really care for princesses, but whenever she does draw one, she's sure to make their skin the perfect shade of brown.

✖ ✖ ✖ ✖ ✖ ✖ ✖

From: Tom ▮▮▮▮▮▮▮▮▮▮▮▮▮▮

To: Damon Young ▮▮▮▮▮▮▮▮▮▮▮▮▮

Subject: Racism Is Really Bad

Hello!

I just read "Racism Is Really Bad," and I have a question to ask you! (If you don't mind!)

When I was eleven years old, a lovely black family ("the Robinsons") moved two doors down from us, making them the first black people on our street. They had two adorable chocolate sons, "Ralph" and "Ronald," and Ronald was close to my age. None of the kids in the neighborhood would play with them, though, and I felt really bad about it. Some days, you'd see Ronald pacing up and down the street, peering into windows with his big brown eyes and sparkling white teeth, hoping that someone would come and toss a football back and forth with him. He even knocked on my door once, and I approached the door, thought about opening it, but instead screamed out, "Nobody's home, blacky," hoping to convince him that no one was home. It didn't work. He just stared at me through the screen door, put his head down, and walked away.

This went on for weeks. Ronald would want to play with us, and we'd ignore him, and he'd go on his porch and cry for hours. Ronald sure had stamina! Once, he even attempted to join a Wiffle ball game we were playing in the street, and as soon as he asked, we all dropped our gloves and bats and went into our houses. It was a coordinated effort, and I felt *terrible*.

Several months or so after the Robinsons moved in, a group of neighborhood kids and I robbed and murdered an old man who lived at the top of our cul de sac. (Mr. Conrad, I think his name was.) He had cash and we wanted it, so he needed to die. Naturally, we framed Ronald for the crime, and he ended up going to juvenile detention and then prison. His family eventually moved too, after we firebombed their station wagon.

Anyway, long story short, fast-forward to the present day. I was browsing Facebook last week, curious about what all the guys from the old neighborhood are doing now, and I found Ronald! He works as some sort of youth pastor or cook or something. He looks great, all things considered. Still has those big brown eyes and that beautiful smile. (And he's still in the city!)

I'm emailing you because I wanted to know if you think it would be appropriate to friend request him. I still feel terrible about everything that happened, and I'd like to buy him a coffee or maybe just send him my favorite scripture. I've read a lot recently about racial microaggressions, and I don't want to cross any lines. Any advice on how to proceed would be greatly appreciated!

Thanks!

Tom

✴ ✴ ✴ ✴ ✴ ✴ ✴

Opening Ceremony; or, Selling Passes to a Wolf Hunt Is *Literally* Selling Wolf Tickets

✳

RION AMILCAR SCOTT

1.

Mayor McJohnson opposed the whole damn thing and with the scribble of a pen could have vetoed the Wolf Hunt, the Declaration of Wolfing, and the official reclassification of all stray and wild dogs as wolves. He could have canceled the opening ceremony, the hunting passes, disinvited the special guests and ordered police to watch over the stray dogs and arrest anyone who even looked at them crooked. Later, he thought of the wolf stews, the wolf barbecues, the men with wolf-puppy skulls around their necks, the proud and fashionable barbarism of the time, and he became filled with sadness, deep regret, and longing to relive the moment of mayoral inaction that allowed it all. But the town council had voted and a vocal minority lobbied and riled everyone up and even those who were disgusted barely raised a whimper until it was too late. He had told himself it was a misplaced bow to civility as a virtue and not cowardice that inspired his blind eye. You pick your battles, he told a reporter. When all was done and a mess of wolf carcasses littered the land and spilled human blood rivaled the flow of the river, his quip became yet another regret. So on that May afternoon, at the top of the opening ceremony, before a crowd of thousands, Mayor McJohnson stood stiff as a statue on that stage while his assistant squirted hand sanitizer onto his outstretched palms. He rubbed his palms together and slowly raised them above his head so everyone could see he had washed his hands of it all. His father, the mayor before him, often did the same thing before executions and all other business he opposed, except he did it with a cauldron of water. His father told everyone the washing of the hands was a tradition that dated back to the Great Insurrection, when bloodthirsty townspeople outvoted the father of Cross River, Maryland, Ol' Cigar, about the whipping and execution of former slavemasters, overseers, and their families. Of course, the original Mayor McJohnson made all that up.

Hand sanitizer worked better than water and soap, the current mayor reasoned. It killed all bacteria. All manner of filthiness. Well, 99.98 percent of it, anyway. Even as he banged the gavel and blew his whistle to great citizenry applause, opening wolf season in Cross River, all blood stained their hands, not his.

2.

Los Lobos performed. As did a female R & B singer named the Wolf Chic, followed by a comedian who'd taken on Wolf as a middle name. The only laughs he earned that day were, unfortunately, at his own expense. But it was the 2nd Amendment Souljahz who caused the vein on Mayor McJohnson's neck to throb. MC Charlton Heston, aka Black Moses, fired a starter pistol into the air. Ronald Ray-Gun, aka FireArmz, gyrated his hips to a throbbing beat and growled the text of the Second Amendment into the microphone.

The mayor stood to the side of the stage gritting his teeth. He said to his assistant, If that nigger shoots off that fucking pistol one more time, you get the police chief on the phone! I'll shut this goddamn farce down!

Black Moses passed the pistol to Ray-Gun, who shot off two

rounds to the song's beat, grinning at Mayor McJohnson in a brazen dare. The mayor balled his fist as if he was about to storm the stage for a good, long brawl, and indeed, he started to say, Thirty years ago I would have kicked that nigger's a—

But a helicopter chopping the air overhead interrupted the mayor. People in the crowd could feel the rhythm of the blades beating deep within their chests. Children and their parents pointed and cheered. It swooped in a circular arc, heading for the Wildlands.

3.

The brown-haired woman holding the rifle grinned and did a thumbs-up to the crowd who looked on from the edge of the Wildlands as she peered down on the clearing from her seat in the helicopter. A pack of dogs, wolves—whatever you want to call them—drank from the river. The copter hovered over them as if suspended by string. She pulled her trigger once. Twice. It had been so long since she hunted this way in her native Alaska. She felt waves of serenity after each shot. But she was also rusty, and a feeling of irritation quickly followed the peace. Bullets flew wide, digging themselves into the earth. The canines scattered. Another bullet and another and another, but the wolves had fled.

4.

Twenty minutes after the helicopter hunt, the gunwoman took to the stage, holding wolf carcasses by the tail. Funny, because she had killed none during her helicopter flight. The carcasses looked stiff, possibly frozen or still thawing. She raised the long-dead animals over her head; the higher she held them, the louder the crowd yelled. She smiled broadly and winked.

You're all patriots, she screamed. I honor these sacred creatures for giving their lives for our nourishment, our warmth. As you all know, I was mayor of a small town in Alaska—Wasilla—not much bigger than this one and I was governor of the whole darn state for a time and one thing the frozen vanilla tundra of my home state has in common with the chocolate hills of Cross Rivers is that we don't take nature for granted. We're one with the hunt, eh? Aren't we? Aren't we?

She paused for the clapping and whistling. Again, she winked at the crowd.

From the wolves and mooses back home in Alaska, to these somewhat smaller wolves here in Cross Rivers, you bet we're gonna keep reloadin' and shootin' like the true Americans we are!

More cheering. Mayor McJohnson, standing next to his assistant by the side of the stage, rubbed his weary eyes with a knuckle and a thumb. This ignorant woman doesn't even know the name of the town, he said.

I don't know, Mayor, his assistant said. She is really quite charming in person. Mayor McJohnson stared blankly at his assistant. Anyway, the mayor's assistant continued. This is not so bad. When have you ever seen broad swaths of the town united?

This is a hate rally. We're the Black KKK and the dogs are our niggers. I wish this nonsense was over with. When do we present the Environmental Education Scholarships to the poor kids?

We don't. The governor's speaking fee ate up a good portion of the event budget.

Detestable, the mayor said. Simply, simply fucking detestable.

The first thing the mayor noticed when the woman stepped from the stage was that the shoulder pads of her bloodred sports jacket made her appear broader than he expected. She was also a tall woman and he had to look up at her. She hunched over when she offered him her hand. Her grip had a heft and a force; it jostled his knuckles beneath the skin, turning his hand into a bag of bones.

Charles, the former governor said. Can I call you Charles? Mayor McJohnson nodded. The former governor's smile faded quickly. She pulled him close and whispered gravely: Charles, I have some concerns I want to share with you.

Not even a *Hiya!*, Madame Governor? the mayor asked.

She watched him with a face of chilled stone. Only a moment, but long enough to send a line of ants marching down Mayor McJohnson's spine.

Please don't treat me like a ninny, Charles. I'm not a ninny, and if you're not a ninny as well you will cancel this whole goddamn thing. In short, this dog hunt your townspeople are perpetuating has the potential to be a catastrophe if not closely controlled and I have seen no evidence of tightly drawn regulatory parameters that will keep this from spiraling into a kind of anarchy. I am a fan of hunting moose and smaller game, but this has the stench of an unmitigated calamity.

With all due respect, Madame Gov—

Before you become defensive, Charles, I think it is in your best interest to peruse this report I took the liberty of drawing up. The governor snapped her fingers and her husband appeared by her side holding a large misshapen brown leather handbag. She reached deep inside and pulled out a thick stack of papers held together with a comb binding under a clear plastic cover.

There are a few flawed equations late in the document, she said—and I promise to send you corrections—but that doesn't change the overall conclusion: this hunt taps into the inherent bestial aspect of mankind and then combines that with our tendency to form unthinking mobs. The damage to Cross River, I must say, will be breathtaking and unprecedented. Some of the more extreme models project casualties deep into the hundreds, possibly low thousands—hundreds of thousands when you factor in the dogs.

Um . . .

Feel free to check all my work. There is an algorithm we used that I'm not sure I stand by, but much like the equations I mentioned earlier, they do not impact my conclusions. I ran this report by some trusted researcher friends at the University of Alaska–Fairbanks. They all—with some concerns noted in appendices one and three—endorsed this work.

Now, Madame Governor, my administration has been a strong voice against the hunt and—

And yet, even with your considerable veto power, it is still happening, Charles. Curious. A little thought experiment, Charles: Say you work closely with a dictator who has murdered and enslaved and oppressed millions. You have been seduced by the power and privilege that being so intimate with this dictator affords you. There is a certain force you now possess. She paused and smirked at him with her head cocked to the right. Because you are fundamentally a good guy, she continued, your conscience has been ranting at you and in a moment of lightning-like brilliance it breaks through, causing you to murder the dictator so he will not inflict any more hurt onto the people. This rare act of humanity ends his regime and frees millions of people from the yoke of oppression. Does this act, this great moment of pure courage, wash your soul clean from all your many years of siding with power against the people?

I don't quite—

You betcha it does! the former governor said. But the masses will never see it that way. Your redemption will remain between you and your God. To the public you will maintain your status as a criminal against humanity. You will be dragged in the street and hung for your crimes. Do you see what I'm getting at here? Mayor McJohnson stared unblinkingly, his face blank and his eyes empty. Charles, she continued, this hunt is your dictator and it matters little that you are opposed to it as long as you keep doing its will. And it does not matter what you do down the road if you do not act before things get bad. Listen to people like your oh-so-foolish council member Anthony Welding and you are dead—morally, politically, spiritually, and maybe even physically. But what do I know? I'm just a hockey mom, right?

Madame Governor, Mayor McJohnson said. If you're so passionately against this as to draw up an extensive report, why come to Cross River and speak in favor of the hunt?

Shucks, Charles, you might as well ask why anyone does anything. The former governor locked arms with her husband and began walking off. It is all about the Benjamins, as some of your great urban philosophers once said. Same reason Welding proposed the hunt. Your town coffers are exploding, right? She turned her head and winked. You would be surprised how people act when money and power are on the table. I am only human, Charles; I am not exempt from that.

5.

The newsman's face glowed a bright pinkish red. He turned his back to the mayor's assistant, grumbling and spitting when he spoke. Then he glared at the young man.

Again, Mr. B——, the mayor's assistant said. I'm sorry if there was a mix-up—

Mix-up! Wolf screamed. I was lied to. I was told this was a celebration of riverbeat music. I'll travel to Cross River any day of the week to listen to some good riverbeat—everyone knows this about me. I grew up watching *Soul Train* and listening to riverbeat. But this is a dog slaughter. A dog genocide disguised as a wolf hunt. You people are sick.

Mr. B——, your outrage is understandable—

Is this because my name is Wolf? Did you invite any other *wolf* celebrities? Where's Warner Wolf? Guess he was smart enough to turn you down, huh?

Please don't be ridiculous. The audience is waiting for your address. Should I tell the people of Cross River that you're disgusted with them? That you said, *You people are sick*?

You snotty little—This is not a race thing. I have every Phoenix Starr album and grew up listening to Dave the Deity, Action Figures, and every other great riverbeat band. After I watched *Soul Train* I'd spin a riverbeat record. Let me tell you, buddy, the Black chicks loved my riverbeat records. Get down there in my parents' basement, put on some Silky Jackson, and you should have seen those Black chicks start to glow. People used to wonder how a skinny, nerdy Jewish guy like me always had a Black chick or two. My uncle in Cross River bringing me riverbeat records every time he visited, that's how. Ha! I was the man. Had the Black chicks going crazy. Black chicks with Afros and butts as thick as I don't know what! Anyway, when I said you people I was referring to the goddamn organizers and all the other liars who booked me.

Look, I had nothing to do with booking you. Mayor McJohnson extends his apologies. The administration, as you know, has been against the hunt and we've been very hands-off with this ceremony. However, there is a loyal majority who are riled up and excited about the hunt. Many of them came to see you and would be disappointed if you didn't make an appearance as planned. I'm obliged to speak for them. Most of the audience are huge fans of cable news and I'm told your show does very well here. And of course, there is a contract in place, so . . .

Where is the mayor anyway? Why couldn't he tell me any of this to my face? You're not pissed he sent you to deal with his mess?

Last I checked he was on the phone with some academics out of Alaska.

Lord, what a mess. I planned to dance around a little bit, say some words about riverbeat, and maybe meet Cliffy2K and Jupiter Starr. Are they here?

No. They think the hunt is barbaric.

Damn it, I was told they'd be performing.

The 2nd Amendment Souljahz performed.

That's hardly riverbeat. That's garbage. Crap. All right. Shit. Are you people really going to hunt stray dogs?

The mayor's assistant nodded.

Have you read the governor's report?

It's a bit over my head.

Mine too. Wolf paused. This is sick. Just sick.

Give it up for yourselves, Maryland! the newsman shouted to the wildly applauding crowd. Give it up for yourselves, Cross River! When I was young, I was the only dude in my neighborhood in Buffalo who knew about Dave the Deity and Action Figures, or how about Bobby Rivers and the Insurrection Band? *Ska-skibby-skibby-she-bop-bop when she walk / Give me dat Cross River funk!*

The newsman stood still, waiting for laughter and applause. For days he'd practiced his ironic riverbeat strut. Such was his love for the music, but the crowd met him only with silence.

Okay, he continued. Who's ready for some hunting?

This time, a cheer, some whistles, and a bit of applause rose from the crowd. The newsman two-stepped a little and paused. He felt the audience now on his side.

You know what I think? I think maybe you should leave the dogs alone. What have they done to you, huh?

A wave of boos passed over the crowd. He raised his arms. All right, he said. Calm down. You're some sick people. You know that?

The crowd's jeering reached a fever pitch. A man in the front row stood and threatened to punch the newsman in the face.

Hey, Wolf replied. Just because you see me on television doesn't mean I won't come down there and kick your ass, buddy.

Wolf and the audience cursed back and forth. A shoe swept past his head. The mayor's assistant dashed onto the stage to rescue the newsman, but before he could reach him, a bottle of Crazy Ninja Malt Liquor struck Wolf in the face, knocking him out cold. The mayor's assistant and several men dragged him backstage while dodging rocks, bottles, and all manner of flying things.

For many years the joke was that a famous newsman was the first Wolf taken out in the hunt.

6.

The opening ceremony had been over for nearly an hour when the mayor crouched in the bush with his son. The hunt interested seven-year-old Donté McJohnson, but so did the wild yellow flowers growing in some nearby brush. Pretty like the ones in his mother's garden. She could never keep them alive for more than a week. The exception was the one Donté had ripped from the root, thinking his act of destruction would help his father eradicate weeds from the garden. His mother flopped down and cried when he showed her what he had done. When Donté thought of that moment, he felt sweat and then warmth at his backside, and then he heard the sound of his father bawling, then his mother slamming her palms down on his exposed flesh. How could such a little mistake cause so much pain?

You listening, Tae? the mayor asked his son. You busy looking around for wolves, but you don't even have the ammunition ready for me. Remember, you my apprentice. You do a good job and we shoot off some rounds together. Okay? But you got to do a good job. Stay aware.

Father and son wore matching jungle fatigues, complete with identical mesh caps and gloves that Donté's mother had spotted in the mall a few days before the hunt. She just had to see her boys in the outfits, she told the mayor.

Chirelle, I ain't wearing that, the mayor told his wife. Bad enough my advisors say I need this photo op. Camera's gon' catch me and my son looking like the only Black dudes on *Duck Dynasty*.

The mayor's wife curled her arms around her husband's torso and looked up at him, sporting a sharp smile.

Mr. Mayor, she said. You're gonna wear those jungle fatigues, 'cause I bought 'em and I say you'll look cute in them, and you're gonna take Donté with you and you'll both be my manly hunting men and you'll smile for the cameras and the whole town'll love you like usual.

What am I supposed to tell Donté after I spoke out against this, huh? What am I supposed to say to my son while we killing dogs?

Chirelle sucked her teeth and released her husband's torso.

Charles, she said. Your seven-year-old son doesn't follow local politics. You'll sit in that bush and you'll tell him about honor, about honoring his responsibilities. If it comes up, you tell him that sometimes he'll have to do things he doesn't want to do just to keep going. You tell him that pictures of the hunt will buy him four more years in this nice big house he loves to live in. Tell him all that.

While they stalked the forest, the mayor told his son some of these things, but Donté kept silent; he couldn't hear his father. All he could hear was yellow. The flowers all around them had deranged his senses. Donté thought he could smell the yellow, a sweet scent distinct from the fragrance of the flowers. The yellow vibrated beneath his feet. The taste of yellow rested on his tongue. He found himself lost in wonder, transported by the blossoms and their rapturous shine. These could replace the plant he'd destroyed, Donté thought, and he reached to pick one. They were better than his mother's flowers. So untamed. So raw in their wildness.

When the story of Donté McJohnson spread about town, it became as wild and as colorful as those flowers. More of a cartoon than something that could happen in real life. This was partly because of how the mayor explained it to authorities and how the newspaper played it.

Mayor McJohnson spoke in a grumble to his son, nearly inaudibly. Lessons on life. Patience. The honor of the hunt, the hunted, and of sport. Honor in general. Being a man. And ironically, he spoke of paying attention. Focus. Focus.

That's how the mayor told it. Later, it became common knowledge that a wolf had curled at Mayor McJohnson's side listening intently to the fatherly message, snickering every few minutes. That wolf, a taunting trickster. More Bugs Bunny than the menace of the Big Bad Wolf. The wolf is a later addition, though.

What the mayor told police was this: Through that one open eye, he saw a blur. And contrary to his lessons on patience and surety, the bush got the better of him. His skin chafed from the itchy flora. His joints ached from barely moving. When Mayor McJohnson saw that blur through the shiny bright flowers, he took a breath and pulled the trigger.

You Ain't Killing That Shit Until a Black Woman Say So

✳

MAHOGANY L. BROWNE

'm not talking about your worth. I'm not even talking about your potential. I'm talking about your swag, your shine, your ability to make the sun hot. It is only in this specific moment of seeing (some lame might think that I mean observing—but this ain't that) that a Black woman will give you the glory required to let you know whatever you did to get up out the house that day—however you made breakfast, or took care of children, or washed up after folks and still walked out the house looking blingy-bright—did not go unnoticed. Because to be noticed while surviving the systemic annihilation stewed into the fabric of this country's consciousness is an act of God. So when a Black woman says, "Okay, boots!," in your chest it feels like the sky opened and diabetes-free chocolate raindrops fell from it just in your honor.

I come from the school of articulation. I learned how to sing a woman sky-high with compliments so she could make it through the rest of the day, her gaze steady on whatever goal lay ahead of her. A woman walking into the grocery store with her big church hat and kitten heels would garner the praise of her sisters-in-arms. A young Angela Bassett receiving a nod from the late great Tina Turner on her impeccable talents. Whitney Houston praising Missy Elliott with two words: "Missy's bad!" Which is to remind one another (despite the white gaze) the tradition of Black-folk testimony is alive and spicy. I reckon I learned this from my mother and aunties. And if you like me, with a grandmother from the South, then you probably learned it from her without even knowing.

Back in Oakland, California, when driving my late grandmother Elsie Jean to CalWest Bank or toward Piedmont for the "wealthy people" fruit options, she would roll the window all the way down, put her arm in the open breeze, and people-watch with the precision of an IRS auditor. Every line item inspected ("If you catch me wearing that, you betta not"), calculated ("If she had just put on a belt"), and—if need be—corrected ("Look at her, baby, you remind me of her. Except . . ."). And I held my breath, because no one can read you to filth like a churchgoing prayer warrior. She finished without a glance my way, "Look at them heels. Now, those are good shoes."

That was the day I realized my knockoffs from Payless Shoe-Source, bought to match my new role as a hospital office clerk, didn't meet the standards of my fly grandmother. I'm telling you I thought I was killing it. My clean pleather shoes, shaped like a flattened boomerang, with a suede belt across the toe tucked smartly by a silver buckle. I ignored the ballerina knockoffs, which were probably more classic and timeless, for this shiny neon-sign pair of 10s screaming *CHEAP! CHEAP! CHEAP!*

Her headscarf whipping in the wind, her nails clean, and her hands crossed over her leather pocketbook. She didn't mean harm, but she wasn't in the business of coddling either. Not when the world outside our front door would penalize me for not "looking" the part. She wasn't in the business of playing it cute when my ability to rise through the ranks in a professional office setting was in question. I took the fast route that day, quick to get her home and get those blaring shoes of regret off my feet. The next paycheck I splurged on a pair of sensibly priced, stylish, square-heeled leather booties from Nordstrom Rack. Upon entering the house, my grandmother looked me from north to south, settled down, and nodded approvingly while singing, "Okay, leather boots."

It's in our lineage. Black women are the epitome of get to it. They tell you when your hair is unpinned and when your buttons are too low. They tell you when you got something in your teeth and when your country is on fire. They know the difference between "Look at the beautiful baby" and "Now, that's a baby!" Don't play with these women. They are the purveyors of the adage "Don't get caught with your slip showing," which is the precursor to "shade."

"Shade" as a verb rather than a place was introduced to me by Jackée Harry during her role on *227*. She would saunter, side-eye, and *tsk* at any missed opportunity to be, well, as fly as she was. Today's shade got claws and fangs and is furious. There was a clear distinction between shade as a form of inquisitive love and playing the dozens.

Playing the dozens could get you dusted in a lunchroom.

Your mama so Black . . .

Your daddy so ugly . . .

Your house so nasty your roaches got roaches . . .

Your Ronald McDonald–ass shoes . . .

And on and on. The slick jokes about family, money, housing, grocery store kicks, and jacked-up haircuts were considered the dozens and to the outside eye were baked in cruelty. But I recognized this form of verbal jujitsu as preparation for how to deal with a classist world that would rather harm you than heal you. I believe however painful those burn sessions were, they prepared me for the boardroom scowls, being passed over for promotions, and missing invitations to elite office gatherings. So, when our foremothers called that shit out, it was square biz. It was less malice and more observation. It was "I will protect you from their unforgiving glances." You can't tell me shade ain't a Black woman's invention. Say something.

Black women be stewards of the good word. And in a world where Black Girl Magic and Black Boy Joy are scrutinized for reducing Black adults to children rather than celebrated for their insistence on Black people's inherent right to happiness, liberation, and expansiveness, it serves as search party and land acknowledgment.

Yes, blouse!

I see you, skirt.

Let's go, baby hairs!

A blouse, or a skirt, or even dexterous waves against the temple might be mostly mundane, but praising them is a salute to the most exquisite small acts of resistance. Don't get it twisted, this ain't no catcall but a neon signal blinking: *Seen. Seen. Seen.*

Sure, I could give you statistics on how many Black girls go missing before the media decides we be worth finding. But Google is free. Besides, I know it to be the truth when I walk out the house not quite feeling myself. My pants feel too bunched up near my thickening thighs. My white leather Chucks are scuffed but at least I got my fave crop top sweatshirt with TUPAC SAVED ME embroidered over my heart. It keeps me feeling grounded. Maybe my homegirl Adelfa, a fellow Black woman writer and mother, made it just for me. Her hand-stitching stole my breath and like all mothers, she gifted me what I didn't know I couldn't live without. A warm piece of cloth made just for me. So when I make my purchases at a local Flatbush beauty supply store, I catch the eye of a young woman, about the same age as my daughter. She's trying to make out the words on my shirt and when she does, her eyes light up. She notices me noticing her and squints as her mouth aims down. I can't tell if she feels shame because I caught her smiling at my statement sweatshirt or if she just hasn't been handed down the *supreme* gift of complimenting Black women.

I don't hesitate. There are plenty of spaces Black girls rarely get to feel safe, soft, and seen. So, offering a bridge that only an auntie would, I go: "Okay, lashes." And she blushes a light so bright it blinds us all.

Baby Wipes

✳

D WATKINS

With a few fresh baby wipes resting on top of the wipe warmer, I pin my baby girl Cross down with my left elbow. Because although I have washed my hands like I'm about to perform neurosurgery on a neurosurgeon, as my sweet wife has instructed, I then touched my iPhone, the device my sweet wife considers to be the dirtiest shit in our home. (Sometimes I wonder if she thinks I rub my phone around the rim of a fucking dumpster every night for twenty minutes before I come in for dinner.)

While trying not to press too hard onto my daughter's torso, I reach for the hand sanitizer. I think of rewashing my hands but don't want to step away while she's on the changing table—she could take a leap of faith deep into her fuzzy pink throw rug and land both of us in the doghouse.

Cross squirms and kicks, knocking the wipes off the warmer, as I punch a perfect glob of sanitizer into the center of my palm. I am sanitized. I try to pull out another wipe, but it's stuck, so I tug. Sixty wipes explode out of the box onto the changing table and the floor.

"You okay up there?" my sweet wife yells from downstairs. "You wash your hands?"

"Yes," I reply, followed by a semi-offended, "You know I washed my hands!"

"Yeah, okay," she answers. "I didn't hear you do it. And remember the CDC recommends forty-five to sixty seconds in lukewarm water!"

Fuck the CDC, I think as I control the task at hand.

Cross is playing with the wipes, tossing them into the air like LeBron does that powder on game nights. I grab a chunk of the remaining wipes off the table with one hand and undo her Pampers with the other. Inside is fifteen pounds of waste that somehow came out of my fifteen-pound baby. *What in the fuck?* The entire second floor of the house now smells like chitlins in a Sunoco urinal.

I power forward, using the remaining wipes to disappear all evidence of the feces, rolling those soiled wipes into her heavy Pampers, then rolling the whole package into a tight ball, sealed at every angle to suppress the funk. I slam-dunk the ball into the Diaper Genie, then quickly apply the regimen of lotions, oils, shea butter, sea moss, black seed oil, and creams that my sweet wife requires after every change, before fastening on a new Pampers. Cross jumps to her feet, still up high on the table, spreading her arms, excited to hug me for completing the task.

"Dad-yeeeee," she says.

"One second, baby," I tell her.

I reach for her shorts and catch a whiff of a toxic odor wafting from a place it should not waft from, because I just cleaned her thoroughly and I know I sealed that diaper with CIA-level security. *What is that smell?*

I look down at my hands. My index and middle fingers have a thick brown swirl of chocolate shit on them that I have also transferred to Cross's shorts. Now I have to take the big gamble of flipping myself into the bathroom to thoroughly wash my hands, while peeking out the door every three seconds to make sure she doesn't jump off the table, then drying my hands, then checking them again, then drenching them in enough sanitizer to make my skin burn and peel and bleed.

I do all of this quickly and efficiently, and then I run a bath to wash Cross as thoroughly as I washed my hands, regreasing her with the same assortment of lotions, and snap on a new Pampers and outfit.

Mission accomplished. This is what being a great father feels like, I think.

Cross smiles, showing off all her tiny white teeth. "Hello, Dad-yeeeeee!"

"Hey, Cross." I smile back. "You shitted on me, baby, but I still love you."

"Shit!" she yells.

"No, baby, don't say that!"

"Don't say what?" my sweet wife asks, walking into the room. She looks Cross over, places her back onto the changing table, yanks off the Pampers, readjusts the tabs, and tells me that I put it on wrong.

"What?" I reply, with a hit of anger. Is my sweet wife trying to snatch away my moment? Can she not see that I'm *Dad-yeeeee*?

"It's not a big deal," my sweet wife says, applying all the lotions and gels and creams I have already applied. "You just have to make sure the bottom is secure. We don't want her leaking out."

Cross gleams and, like a traitor, gives my sweet wife the hug that was meant for me.

I get upset like a child. I don't yell or scream or shoot back rebuttals. I am more of an inside-my-head type of guy. Deep, deep into my skull is where I venture, to the section responsible for questions like: *What does she mean I didn't put the diaper on right? Does she know I've changed this little girl's diaper a zillion times? Does she know my fingers were just covered in shit, and I still was able to save our daughter from becoming one with that shit? Could she not smell the 172 lotions I applied in the order she told me to apply them? Does she know that I care just as much as she does? Does she think that I don't care? I bought this girl multiple pairs of off-white Nikes when plenty of pairs of Pumas and them dumb-ass-looking Filas were available, so how could I not care? Why does she think that I don't care?*

All my dad had to do, literally, was show up.

I grew up in the eighties, at the height of the crack era. Many of the dads from my neighborhood were on the wrong side of the drug war: using them, selling them, sitting in a box because of them, or dead.

Having a dad was rare; in the event of the miracle of your dad being present, then that nigga was either bitterly insufferable because of what society does to Black men, or you probably only saw him on holidays. Present dads lived at work; they made money, came home, fed the family, relaxed with a beer for every bit of two minutes, and then got up and went to work again. They didn't change Pampers, give feedings, or wrap their fingers in baby shit like me. No dealing with emotional growth and working through the issues that many children face. Dads saw their kids when they saw them.

My dad was there. He had his struggles with drugs and addiction, like many of the men in my neighborhood when I was young, but he always kept a job and made sure we had the basics: food, shelter, Nikes. His presence made him a local hero, but the lack of paternal figures also set expectations extremely low. All my dad had to do, literally, was show up.

Sometimes I fuck with him. "I swear your generation was terrible," I say with a laugh. "You niggas weren't responsible for anything except money. You niggas didn't even know your children's names!"

These days, being a good dad means taking your kid to school every day, mastering all kinds of stupid TikTok dances, making a bunch of money no matter how fucked up the economy is, wearing a bunch of Balenciaga, being a master photographer and social media caption writer, and cooking five-star meals, perfectly plated and photographed, to receive no fewer than one thousand likes after the first two hours on Instagram. I'm exhausted.

My dad often reminds me that his dad—a drunk, philandering salesman and alleged war vet—wasn't around, so he had no real example of what a *great father* would be.

"You know I try my best?" my dad once asked. "You know I tried to be the father you needed."

"You did good, my nigga," I responded. "The best father I could ever ask for."

He choked up, his eyes becoming glossy wet slits as he pulled me in for a hug. That's also rare, because I don't really hug, but I obliged him. I was being 1,000 percent honest. As far as dads went, he was the best I ever saw. Of course I could give my father a rundown of his mistakes, just as my daughter will be able to count mine. But despite his flaws, I still think he is amazing.

What will my daughter think of me?

Will I be the best in her eyes or a fucking dud? Times are changing. The era of the absent Black father is over.

Not only are statistics showing a rise in the presence of minority fathers in households, but we Black fathers are also working hard at being the people our fathers could not be for us. My friends who are dads are not only spending time with their children, they are getting their nails painted, baking cupcakes, figuring out how to braid hair, and loving every minute.

According to the CDC, who earlier I said "fuck them" about, "Black fathers are more likely than their white and Hispanic counterparts to feed, eat with, bathe, diaper, dress, play with, and read to their children daily." We are being more vulnerable, fighting to be more understanding, and sharing chores with our spouses, while doing the emotional work and trying our best to be as present with our children as mothers have been for generations. But are we doing it right? After all, I thought I did a good job on that diaper, but I put it on wrong. What else am I doing wrong while aimlessly thinking I'm doing a good job? Am I not strapping her tight enough into the car seat? Does she wear too much Fear of God for a two-year-old? Am I putting too much cinnamon in her oatmeal?

"Are you a good father?" I asked one of my close friends. "What does your lady think? Better yet, what does your little kid think?"

"I swear, bro, I ask myself that all the time," he responded. "I feel like I am, but you know, I might be pretty fucked up, you know . . ."

I do know. It's hard to gauge your impact when you are present every day and the results don't really come in until you get to see your child's grade school, collegiate, or business accomplishments; their fashion choices; the impact they have on the people around them and their community; the way they interact with their own family (if they decide to have one); and then the ultimate test: how they reflect on their childhood. What will she say about me?

Will my daughter say that I was the most loving and caring guy she ever met, a true gift from God? Or will she say, "This nigga couldn't even change my diaper without dipping his fingers knuckle-deep in baby shit! Get this dickhead out of here!"

But it could be worse.

My daughter could become an annoying antivaxxer who talks about Bitcoin, NFTs, and motherfucking Black excellence all day. She could be broke and owe niggas. She could be a YouTube-educated flat-earther. She could be internet woke and wear them weak-ass revolutionary graphic tees from Urban Outfitters. What if she came in my house with Team Jordans on? This shit could get ugly.

My sweet wife snaps me out of my Aquarian aloofness by questioning my constant daydreaming: "What are you thinking about?" she asks.

"Nothing," I say instead of telling her that my inability to change a Pampers perfectly, two years in, makes me feel like a loser, like the nigga they kicked out the Five Heartbeats. In these moments my sweet wife always responds Maya Angelou–ish with something like "You are beyond amazing, king! The only patriarch that could lead us to the promised land, as you stand on the shoulders of the ancestors and divinity!" but isn't she supposed to say that? I can't imagine her actually saying, "Our daughter would truly be better off if you spent more time at work. As a matter of fact, take a job in another city and Zoom in biweekly, because things are better when you aren't around."

I sit with all of these rambling thoughts and ideas—sometimes while holding my daughter, sometimes while the three of us are curled up together on the couch, the two of them fast asleep. In those moments, I can't help but feel like I did something right. The intimacy allows me to pull away from the emotions that cloud this journey, and I can see that I am not special, and neither is my wife or her comments on how I administer care. Because the truth is there will be times my sweet wife will get it wrong too, and I know she cares more than anything. And if I'm lucky, I will be there to pick up the pieces the same way she fixed the lopsided Pampers. This is what family is.

We are normal people who are sharing a beautiful experience, and what is special is the way we live, love, try, and talk about that experience, for us and for the sake of our child, her life and well-being.

We love our union and our child dearly and will proudly suit up and go to war over that love with anyone and everyone—but that should not mean each other.

I watched my sweet wife change our daughter a few times after our exchange. Carefully and slowly, I mastered her artful technique, her ability to throw multiple wipes in the air with her left hand and catch with her right, without even looking, before sanitizing our child. I vowed never to walk away from the changing table until my daughter's diaper was applied a step beyond perfect, in a manner that exceeded the company's application guidelines and expectations.

With all of this bullshit behind me, I finally felt good enough to earn my sweet wife's respect and even had the confidence to change my daughter in front of a loud judgmental audience.

"Nigga, no, no, take that Pampers off of her," my sweet wife said after I finished changing my daughter. "Do you listen? We not using Pampers anymore, we switched to Pull-Ups."

Crowd Work

✳

ROY WOOD JR.

My first television credit was *Showtime at the Apollo*, in 2001. They had this head-to-head competition show called "Comedy TKO." Which was unprecedented, because up until then they'd only allowed comedians to compete on amateur night—a sucker's bet for comics since you're going up against actual singers. And kids. You can't beat a cute kid who's singing "Greatest Love of All." You can't even beat an ugly kid who's singing "Freek'n You."

But as *Showtime at the Apollo* evolved, they finally understood. Comedy was just never going to beat singing or kids. Which is why so many comics who performed there got booed off the stage. It was rigged against us!

Okay, amateur night is amateur night, but we have to separate the children from the amateurs, and we have to separate the comedians from everyone else.

That said, the comedian who I believe had the biggest upset at the Apollo—or probably the best set of anyone I've ever seen there (and I'm including Mo'Nique)—is Gabriel Iglesias. And I know part of that is because he's a big dude. And I think that there's something with us—and by "us" I mean "niggas"—in that if you a big boy, we don't see you as a threat. Especially if you're not Black, because we assume you must be courageous to get in front of a bunch of niggas to tell jokes. I'd even argue that non-Black comics who do "urban" comedy get more leeway than we do.

Anyway, so "Comedy TKO" is announced. And every comedian is chomping at the bit to get on. *Showtime at the Apollo* used to come on every Sunday night in Birmingham on UPN 68, and I'd watch it and just sit there and talk shit about whichever comedian was on. Which really was just hate because I wanted what they had. And this was at a time when it seemed like everyone was booking Black comics on TV. This was the peak of BET's *ComicView*. Well, maybe not the peak. But they were at a cruising altitude and had already made stars of Sommore and Ced the Entertainer and D. L. Hughley. The Kings of Comedy had already happened. But everyone thought that the next Kings of Comedy were yet to be discovered. And that you needed a TV credit to give yourself some credibility.

The way I looked at it was if I could get on *Showtime at the Apollo*, then I could get on *ComicView*. And if I killed *ComicView*, then I'd book *Def Comedy Jam*. And if I killed *Def Comedy Jam*, I'd meet Ice Cube. And then he'd put me in a movie. And then if Ice Cube put me in a movie, I'd meet Nia Long. Which was my ultimate goal. 'Cause I still associated her with Brandi from *Boyz n the Hood*. Which means I still thought of her as Cuba Gooding Jr.'s girlfriend. And I was pretty sure I could whoop Cuba's ass, which meant she would date me. And then I could retire and build a house for my mama and Nia Long.

So I finally sent a three-minute tape to *Showtime at the Apollo*. I don't remember the jokes I told, but I remember they were decent enough. This was October. Maybe November. A couple months pass without a reply, so I get back to talking shit. About the show, the comics, the Apollo, Harlem, Harlem niggas, Adam Clayton Powell—basically anything associated with that place. But then the morning of January 3, I get a call.

"How you doing, Roy? It's Ben Hill. I'm the talent producer for *Showtime at the Apollo*."

I start shaking in my boots, and I speak to him like we're in the marines.

"Yes, sir, Mr. Hill, sir."

"We would like to invite you to be on the new season of *It's Show-time at the Apollo*, hosted by Rudy Rush and Kiki Shepard."

I'm in shock and can't speak, so he speaks again.

"Well, Roy. Can you do the show?"

"Yes, sir. I can, sir."

Then Hill politely explains that there is no travel or hotel budget, and there is no per diem. The only thing he can guarantee is a microphone and two thousand people ready to hear what I have to say. Later that day I hear from my Memphis homie Henry Coleman that he's just been invited too, so we make a plan to travel to New York together, since neither of us has ever been there. Two bitter-ass, Mad Rapper–ass comics from the South, planning to caravan to Harlem together. What could go wrong?

We search for affordable hotels, and we find one—the Knights Inn in Elizabeth, New Jersey, for $37 a night. We should've known then what we were getting into, but we didn't know jack shit about hotel costs and accommodations. Plus, in the South, $37 ain't always a terrible room. Okay, it usually is terrible. But not murder terrible.

We drive up to New York a few days before the show to get comfortable and practice our sets. We get to the Knights Inn and *oh my god*. There were open-air drugs. Sold and used. There were sex workers all through the parking lot. It was a horseshoe-shaped motel too, so you could see every car going in and out through the same entrance. I had Alabama plates and Henry had his Tennessee plates and we're already kind of getting looked at a little sideways. But we're young— twenty-one and twenty-two years old—so we're chillin'. We'd go into the city to rehearse at the Apollo, and on the way to our cars the sex workers would give us a nod. And when we'd come back home for the night, they'd nod at us again. They were basically a hotel concierge service.

The day of the show, as Henry and I were walking to the car, one of the sex workers came over to us in a very calm and polite manner.

"Are y'all the police?"

"No."

"Well, why are y'all here? I've watched y'all go in and out of that room for the last three days. What are you doing here? You ain't bought no dope and you ain't bought no pussy. So what's your business while you in town?"

"We're comedians here to tape *Showtime at the Apollo* tonight."

After we said that, a sparkle came into her eyes, and she started giving us the advice that I think she wished she could have been given when she was our age. *Follow your dreams. Keep working hard. Be kind to yourself.* I guess she saw something positive in us. Especially since we clearly looked like schoolboys. Our shirts had collars, and ain't nobody wearing collared shirts in Elizabeth, New Jersey, at one in the morning. She even hollered at the other sex workers.

"These boys tell jokes. They about to go on the Apollo. They about to be famous."

Now, what they don't tell you about the Apollo Theater is that, before you get onstage, everyone in the crowd has been drinking. For *hours*. Also they shoot the show out of order. The night that we performed, they were taping three episodes, so that's three one-hour programs.

The artists performing before amateur night that evening were P. Diddy, Ja Rule, and DMX, and each of them did two songs. So, you literally start the night with the hottest musicians in the country singing the hottest songs at the peak of their careers. And then . . . us. No wonder we got booed.

My show taped before Henry's show, and I went head-to-head against a comedian from Miami named Dexter Angry. Dex goes out and crushes it. I go out and I just do aight. Not terrible. Aight. The sets are supposed to be three minutes long. But at the two-minute-and-forty-second mark, I hear a small smattering of boos. So I decided to cut my set short. Because fuck that, I'm not going to get *booed* booed.

As I walk offstage, the band starts playing. And Ben Hill is backstage, motioning for me to get back out there. I'm like "No, I'm not going to. You're not going to make me stay onstage, bro. I'm getting the fuck off this stage." But Ben Hill is Ben Hill, and sure enough, I bust a U-turn, and now it's me, Kiki Shepard, and Dex onstage. When she put her hand over my head it was like they had extra boos in their pockets that they didn't hit me with the first time. They conjured new boos from the ether. They wanted to make it clear that Dexter Angry was the winner that night.

I finally get backstage, and in the greenroom is every amateur night contestant for the evening. Between the comedians, the unknown R & B groups, and the Apollo Kids, there were like thirty people in there. And when I walked into that room, they all gave me a round of applause. It's still the warmest, most sincere appreciation for a performance that I've ever received from any group of people. Because you knew you were getting applauded by people who understood what just happened up there.

Forty minutes later, Henry goes on. His first joke works. His second doesn't. Someone boos. Before I continue, you should also know that at the Apollo, the crowd is practically right on top of you. The televised shows give the illusion that the room is bigger and wider than it actually is, but in reality it's tight and packed and can get claustrophobic as fuck if you're bombing. It's like a high school auditorium where you can see every face in the room.

I don't know who booed Henry, but he looked directly at that motherfucker and told him to shut up. With comedy—particularly with a comedy contest show—you're screwed if you deviate from your act, because these two- and three-minute sets are constructed and orchestrated down to the second. And once you break that wall with the audience, you're completely fucked, because you're relinquishing your bully pulpit and handing them the power by showing them that they've gotten to you.

From that moment on, the boos just rained down on poor Henry. After maybe ten seconds of that, he put his head down for a moment, lifted it back up, said, "You all don't give anybody a chance. What's the point of even coming up here? You know, fuck y'all." And then this nigga *threw his microphone into the crowd* the way a tennis player would throw a racket. He just threw a hard-ass sound stick into an audience. And it was vile. I wish I could remember exactly what he was saying to those people. But it was high-octane. So high-octane that when Henry came back downstairs into the greenroom, no one clapped.

I wanted to stay and watch the rest of the show, but Henry wanted to dip. So we left. And halfway back to Elizabeth, we both started crying in the car like Carl Thomas, thinking that we came all the way up to New York just to end our careers before they even started.

When we got back to the hotel, the same sex worker who talked to us before we left was sitting there on a car. When she saw us, she started clapping and hollering for us, but she could tell by our faces that it didn't go well. It went the Apollo way. In that moment, she flipped a switch, from encouraging fan to nurturing mother.

"Y'all did good. Don't worry about it. They stupid. Y'all gonna be all right."

I nodded and said thank you and we went to our room. When we got there, Henry started packing immediately.

"Where you going?"

"I'm getting the fuck out. I'm going to Memphis."

"Tonight?"

"Tonight."

We shook hands, and that was that.

An hour later, I went to the vending machine. Which was outside, since this was the Hotel from Hell. The same sex worker was still there.

"You know, baby, some nights I love what I do."

"What do you mean?"

"Well, it's not often, but some nights I actually don't mind having sex. And it's cool to get paid for it. But I don't mind having sex. But sometimes I have to suck a dick with bumps on it."

Now I was just in shock, but trying not to look shocked, because I could sense she was about to drop some serious knowledge. And she did.

"Every now and then, you gonna have to suck a dick with bumps on it. But I promise you, the better you get at this, the fewer dicks you have to suck. And you might actually enjoy what you do from time to time."

And then she walked off. If she'd had a mic, it would have been dropped. It's still the best advice I've ever been given.

Can a Bitch Just Have a Miscarriage in Peace?

✳

HILLARY CROSLEY COKER

I n 2019, I was pregnant, and then in 2019, I was not. Life is cruel but it's got a sick sense of humor and my dumb ass didn't know enough *at first* to laugh. I just . . . went back to work?

Miscarriages are wild things, especially if your only experience losing a child is on purpose. And thanks to the morning-after pill in the early 2000s, which literally felt like a chemical peel of my uterus and wheel of fortune of hormones, I was child-free through college and my twenties. By the mid-aughts, though, I wound up having to take a somber train ride and walk to New York City's famed Planned Parenthood by the old DKNY mural with my then-boyfriend. I loved him, but both of us knew we didn't want any kids together then, or maybe not ever, because getting head while balancing on your actual head with your legs split open is fun but, like, should having an orgasm be this hard? Why are we effectively lifting up all of the couch cushions looking for my g-spot? The Dutty Wine wasn't *actually* made for this.

And then I was a grown-up trying to get pregnant and I did, easily. In fact, when the at-home pregnancy test confirmed I was going to be a *really responsible* adult, I hopped on my bike, rode to Afropunk, and bought purple lipstick, because fuck it, I was really grown now and how much longer would I be able to ride and buy unprofessional lippies?

And then there was the second time I tried to get pregnant. And I did. Until I wasn't. It was a mundane Tuesday morning. My son was three and I'd already dropped him off at school. As I drove to my marriage therapy couples session to talk to a stranger tasked with ensuring that I didn't murder my husband for upholding the patriarchy in the feminist marriage that he signed up for, I began to have what seemed like my period but clearly was not. Because, again, I'm pregnant. Suddenly I realized what was happening and I called my therapist and said, "Sorry, I can't make this morning's session. I've got to go to the emergency room, I think I'm having a miscarriage." My therapist grimly said, "Okay," and offered his condolences. I thanked him. I was in shock. I'd never been here before. *The irony,* I thought, *the fucking irony. I spent my teens and twenties trying not to get pregnant and here my Black ass is, wanting to get pregnant on purpose, and look at me. Driving to work and bleeding out my baby.*

This is some bullshit.

Then my husband came to meet me in the ER, where I'd been accessorized with a giant hose-size needle in my arm that the nurse who stabbed me failed to mention was never coming out, leaving me with an open wound with tape all over it so they could draw blood for the fifty-eleventh time to confirm I'm less of a woman, and definitely not a mother of *two* kids. I laughed to myself, thinking, *Nah, girl,* in Lionel Richie's voice from the intro to "Just to Be Close to You." *Maybe you're a one-and-done girl. But you didn't want to be, you've planned on three kids. What happened? You conceived your first kid so fast. And now here you are, late to work, and texting your boss that you've had a personal emergency but to keep the production train running there, while your ass is sat here, in the ER, waiting to hear the inevitable bad news.*

Suddenly I'm really tired. Exhausted. I know what the doctor is going to say and I want to leave but . . . this damn water hose is still plugged into my left arm, giving me a garish purple bruise.

Finally, after an hour or two, a male doctor tells me I've had a missed abortion. First of all, they have types? And to be honest, a missed abortion feels like an additional stab to the gut where I've already begun cramping. This doctor says that I'll continue to bleed out and there's nothing for him to remove and whatever my body has will pass naturally, okay?

Well, no.

And I sort of crumple into tears in the crowded room of other people having their own life-changing situations as my husband, who is standing beside me, puts his hand around my shoulders. It kind of feels like a subway meltdown, where your hot tears go on to become someone else's story to a friend over drinks. Like, "Girl, why was I on the 2 and this girl was *bawling* into the window? Made me think about *my life.* Poor thing, hope she's all right . . ."

And just like that, my current Valentine's Day is shot and my future ones are forever marked—wait . . . did I mention this happened Valentine's Day morning? It is fucked and I should just go home and lie down but I am in shock, and what do overachiever, busybody professional Black girls do when the chips are down? We go to work like maniacs, propped up by the Strong Black Woman trope and the omnipresent spirit of capitalism. So into my car I go, with a big Band-Aid over that reddish-purple blood-hose bruise. Do you know I worked a full day, editing unimportant-in-the-grand-scheme-of-things things while my uterus was giving up the literal ghost and my brain was shorting out every hour or so, flashing back to all the blood, the realization that I was no longer the mother of a second baby and just . . . what *the fuck* just happened?

Think about that though: I just had a miscarriage and my silly ass went to work. *What is wrong with me?* Welcome to the adventures of a Black woman doing too much and succeeding. And I was doing too much at home too.

I'm married to a gorgeous Jamaican and Gambian man with a delicious ass, who was raised to be an ally to women in his mind but not with his actions. And then he met me, the most outspoken, foul-mouthed, take-no-shit African American woman he could find, who didn't understand that he was actually *serious* about reenacting that cultural alpha male West Indian–African foolishness until he committed to the role at home. And after three years of shouldering most of our household and childcare duties alone and reenacting my own cultural example of a single mother doing it all—y'all, why was I doing that to myself? I was married!—I said, "We have to go to therapy before I pop up on *Snapped* because you're unironically telling me Don Draper lines like 'I don't think about *cleaning the house at all.*' Nigga, then who's supposed to think about it—*just me?!* Ain't no magical invisible housecleaning fairies in this bitch! Who do you think you're talking to?!" And this is all happening between his boys' trip to Puerto Rico after spending half the month traveling for work. So, it was therapy for him or prison for me—and to the couch we went.

The next week after my traumatic ER jaunt I am still bleeding, showing up as a gray shadow of myself. I look in the mirror and laugh. *Come on, Casper, you're getting on your own nerves. Just cook the thing, wash the kid, put him to bed, get him up, care about work, and then come your bedtime, tap* out. I'm bloody-knuckling it through every day because I don't know that miscarriages can last two weeks or more, producing the heaviest period you've ever had in your life plus readjusting hormones. I was a mess, a Picasso mashed into a Basquiat. Suddenly it's Tuesday again and the husband and I go to our therapy session. The Miscarriage is the Topic and my husband says the right things and I guess so do I. We are grieving while parenting a small child who has no idea what we're dealing with, and we won't tell him to protect him. It is horrible.

Two weeks later and I'm still tired, irritable, and pretending everything is fine at work. I'm in the middle of working with HR to fire an employee who we've realized was trying to trade company access in exchange for personal projects with someone named Bayou Bussy. Yep. To be fair, Bayou Bussy is a solid artist and I like her work, but I have to admit the hilariousness of my *management demands* to have to fire someone over trying to scam somebody named this name.

Clearly, I am a very *serious* person.

HR says I've got to read my team member's work emails to see if they've done this before. I like being a manager but now I feel like a narc, a tired narc who's still spotting and wondering when I'll get my body back from the walking graveyard it's become. I'm just fully going to work while in my mind's eye I'm cosplaying Jack from *The Nightmare Before Christmas,* internally screaming, *What's this?!*

I do all of this ruminating between reading emails about, among other things, *SELLING UNDERWEAR ONLINE AT WORK.*

I want to run away.

I am scarred for life. I am discussing the legality of all of this with HR because numerous other things have led up to this moment and this is the final straw but I can barely stand up to finish the conversation.

THEM: Are you OK?

ME: Yeah, just having a miscarriage.

THEM: OMG, Hillary, do you need to go home?

ME: Probably, but let's just sort out this Bayou Bussy thing . . .

How long exactly does shock last before it becomes grim sarcastic jokes?

It's three weeks later, and I'm bleeding less but my emotions are still whirling. I feel like a black cloud of chaos that I'm doing my best to conceal. I pretend I'm fine with my son as I get him up for school, drop him off, and then keep up the façade for work, but after the last meeting and my son's bedtime, I curl into a ball and try to disappear. Then one day, I come home and find my husband on the floor. He says he's thrown out his back, and I'm *incredibly annoyed.* Our son is visibly upset; he doesn't know what's wrong with his father. Meanwhile, my partner is sprawled out and asking for help. My annoyance becomes straight anger because . . .

YO.

CAN A BITCH JUST HAVE A MISCARRIAGE IN PEACE? CAN I FINISH BLEEDING BEFORE THIS MAN HAS SOME MANU-FACTURED CRISIS THAT COULD'VE BEEN AVOIDED WITH SOME DAMN STRETCHING AND A SHAUN T VIDEO? HE BET-TER TILT, TUCK, AND TIGHTEN AND TRULY GET THE FUCK OUTTA HERE WITH THIS "EMERGENCY"!

Four weeks later, I retell this story to my therapist during my solo counseling session and he's in stitches. Obviously, I've won couples therapy and he is On My Side. I'm literally grieving the loss of something dying inside me, going to therapy so you can see that I'm a human being in this relationship *with you,* I say, and we need to raise this kid and work this household *together* after I've been keeping it running forever damn near alone, and the one time I need to regroup, the one fucking time I need to downshift, *you're on the floor? You? Really?* You couldn't wait a few months to fall apart? I couldn't just have a fiscal quarter to heal from this literal internal mess before you had some preventable crisis?

But unfortunately, this is marriage. This is life. This is it.

After the husband heals, we get into a disagreement about something else and I say, "I'm still tired from my miscarriage," and he says something like, "That was forever ago."

I see red and honestly, now I can't remember what was said, but it ends with me sending him to his mother's house with our son so I don't have to look at my partner's face for at least forty-eight hours. I keep our judgmental bulldog, thereby splitting childcare and designating someone to cuddle with during my multihour *Avengers* screening in complete darkness in our small brownstone basement apartment. It's grim. So I start workshopping stand-up material for a friend who's a comedian because what am I supposed to do with all of this humor I keep thinking of? My friend told me to perform them myself, which I did not, but I'll share them with you, because the world is a stage.

MY MISCARRIAGE STAND-UP SET

So I'm married, and I've got one son and he's a bursting ball of fucking energy that I'm trying to give the space to grow into an amazing Black man if the police and white fanaticism don't kill him first. What's white fanaticism? Well, white supremacy is not actually a thing, right? Those people believe in Disney-like fantasies and then twist the United States into a ball to make them happen. Still doesn't make it real, fam! Still a fantasy! Anyway, I'm married to a Jamaican and African man who thinks he's helping at home and at work; I'm managing a team of five millennials and keeping up with every famous rapper and singer's life because I do entertainment news. *I also was pregnant until recently, when I had a "missed abortion," which basically means your body has something dead inside that it's trying to expel on its own while you pretend to be a normal human in meetings and at Target. It's brutal, but keep it sunny! Right? Right.*

But for real, a bitch is tired. I'm tired of being a mom. I'm tired of being a wife. I'm tired of being a career woman. I'm tired of being a boss. I'm tired of being a keeper of the culture. I'm just tired. Then when I tried to rest, because, again, I'm married and my husband should be holding me down and splitting this life shit, he has some ridiculous injury that was just born of his general refusal to help himself be healthy until he falls apart and honestly, WTF. I'm bleeding out from this fucking miscarriage and working hard to pretend that nothing is happening at work so I can fall apart at home, right, and then I come home to this dude lying on the floor with the dog's butt in his face. Can I finish having my miscarriage before you fall apart from something you could've prevented? Read the room, my guy, this isn't the best time.

You know what? I think it's all bullshit, being married. It's supposed to be an equal partnership but it's eighty-twenty, maybe seventy-thirty at best. At fucking best. I'm working full-time, and I mean twenty-four hours a day, managing the men at my job and the men at home. Shit, even my dog is a man! This human bitch is tired!

So, you know what? I'm switching the tables. If I'm doing all this shit, I need my husband to fuck me so good that I forget about all of the things he doesn't do. I am asking to be dickmatized. Treat me like my college and twenties ne'er-do-well paramours who weren't shit but ate my pussy like it was serving breakfast and it was so beautiful that I cried as I handed them a napkin. Give me "Harlem Nights Sunshine" dick! Give me "Moonlight Trevante Rhodes looking at his old boo" dick. I need "Olivia and Fitz Scandal, that shit that only makes sense because of the dick" dick. And then I can forget that I shop, cook, clean, pay the bills on schedule, and organize our entire lives to keep us all alive while working full time because your bedroom eyes allow me to live in your strengths, the strength of you pummeling my pelvic floor into sublime submission and giving me orgasms so strong that I float into the atmosphere. That is the feminism I want. It's why Shirley Chisholm ran for president! Why Florynce Kennedy peed on Harvard's lawn! Why Ida B. Wells fought for women's right to vote! Girl power, I am woman, hear me roar . . . with a giant orgasm that wakes the baby and makes the dog bark, like, "Bitch, I'm trying to sleep!"

Love and Water

✳

LADAN OSMAN

On Valentine's Day in the second grade, I got my first love letter and a sack of chocolates. This little boy went on to propose in each of our elementary years, offering his love confessions theatrically, on bended knee. I don't think I ever said no but I couldn't say yes, so I'd usually run away. If our early romantic encounters mark us, I first experienced fortune. Only a few classmates liked me but those were intense and sincere crushes. We shared food and pencil cases, or walked home together, pausing to check on a cocoon. The next love letter was on the last day of eighth grade. That boy handed it to me trembling and crying, so unembarrassed his friends forgot to mock him. I wasn't ready to go out with anyone. I ended my reply with a nineties gem, and still mean it: *Never change.*

I was a late bloomer. Even through senior year of high school, I wasn't inclined to kiss or hand-hold or lie so I could be alone at the movies with someone nice. I made an early investment in yearning: long looks across a classroom and letters that included drawings or a four-leaf clover pressed inside. A born lovergirl. My mother says it's because she ate too much cake while pregnant with me and went to the beach every day. I wonder if those earnest yet infrequent crushes shape my expectations, my stamina, today. If kids were mean to signify adoration, I didn't notice. There was no ambiguity, no competition, no rejection. It was all love and no war, a steady warmth that remained if we saw each other again as teens. *You're unrealistic,* an ex said in my late twenties. *You're like a* 1001 Nights *character.* My parents never read me fairy tales, and largely banned Disney for political reasons. Most of my ideas about princesses and happily-ever-after are secondhand. Atmospheric. I don't agree with that ex but he had some points. Real life can be coarse. Our teacher made me share that bag of chocolates so everyone got two or three and told a child on the day of his would-be engagement that all Valentine's Day cards must be equal in size and intention. What a hater. Also, my classmate's mom was by the door watching her son's first proposal. Maybe that was a little weird.

As I approached womanhood, I tried to adapt to others' ideas of maturity. I memorized platitudes: play it close to the vest, be hard to get, nice guys finish last. These strategies were useless for my bookish childhood but cynicism seeped in. The pre–reality show, early-internet days of my youth were characterized by searching. Knowledge wasn't so available or private. We had to make do with eavesdropping and a collage of lyrics, movie scenes, and tall tales shared by girls who smoked in school bathrooms. *I can't afford to be soft,* I chanted to myself. Life was about surviving, securing assets, and not getting played by the one man you chose to love. I had crooked teeth and no hope of cleavage before at least twenty-two (an estimate based on old family photos); I needed to focus if I was going to become a bitchy writer who wears vampy lipstick by age forty. One day, I overheard an aunt saying all women need to keep a packed bag hidden away: *Your papers, your gold, and a dress you can't stand to leave behind.* Yes, I thought. I remember it clearly because it was the day Mike Tyson bit Evander Holyfield. I guess two people chewed that day.

I became tactical about love. I had a plan, a *Waiting to Exhale*–infused attitude and color palette. But there was another, conflicting element to my personality: feral, goonish curiosity. I wanted to know what happened next. I needed to see for myself, my gut and logic screaming *HELL NO.* Naturally, I married my prom date. We had nothing in common. We didn't get along. I couldn't compose vows to him, which he used as an excuse to launch a years-long skepticism about my writing. I knew from the beginning it would end. The same sense of knowing that nurtured my solitary playtime, or led me to quirky and sweet friends, attended me like a companion: *You know better, you must leave.* So I did. But for six years I was present yet smug, full of solutions yet always at a loss, aloof yet overbearing. My inner compass was spinning. It was a chaotic exit, my desire to leave clarifying danger. He suggested he'd shoot us both as I was putting on my black Air Forces to go to work. *Well, you'll have to shoot me in my back like Selena,* I said, inadvertently adding another "s" to the end of her name like in the movie. I said those words and don't understand why; can't fully assess my rage, grief, fear, refusal, and Somali-woman humor. From that afternoon on, it was like driving with all the lights timed to green. I found an apartment, packed up my books and clothes, and left one morning. Even aspects of the dissolution were peaceful. The imams I feared would judge me instead prayed for me. The light was golden and diffuse through white curtains that moved with a breeze that nearly made me fall asleep. The scholar said: *May you attain the things you want, which are not wrong, and not too much for God,* and I was freed emotionally, legally. They backdated their ruling. What a gift: they rewound time so I could speed into my future.

Years before my divorce, I met and drew close to someone who walked into my garden and found it without walls. Everything happened between us, and nothing happened between us. Not that it mattered. My ex had a murky relationship with a woman he had all up and through my house. *Nothing happened,* she reassured me. *Remember the floppy-haired rich guy at my garden party?* she babbled in a panic when I called the number dotted all over the phone bill like Morse code. *I want him. He has a boat.* Ironically, of the people I've mentioned, he's the only one I'm connected to on Instagram. He's a wife guy who reads interesting books and offered to teach me how to sail. Anyway, back to the man in my garden. We never dated but our shorthand conversations and mutual warmth, along with the way he was able to transmit affection beyond space or time with his eyes, broke me open and reconfigured me. It wasn't falling in love. It was becoming love. This recognition was paired with melancholy: to be helpless yet safe, to experience a spark discernible to yourself and others, to *dive lightly, lightly* into the stranger, as Mahmoud Darwish wrote. I've seen the thing that made poetry necessary; now what?

There were no mirrors or projectors between us. We were two suns, and as such, orbiting but never touching. I was naked, without armor, and pleased that I didn't need any. For years, I've struggled with the meaning of this connection. The injustice of bad timing, our individual catlike behaviors, my logic overriding my soul, letting each other go, eight years of silence, a weepy conversation last summer that proved our dreams and sense of each other were evidences of an ongoing communication. This, despite the reality that he's happily partnered. Ours is a love for which there's no container. A friend's mom says some lovers leave footprints. When I consider a decade or so of breakups, I remember these Tomaž Šalamun lines: *You never walked on my grass, / don't ever think you did. / Only on the wall. / On top of the wall. / On the bottom of the wall. / On the left side of the wall. / On the right side of the wall. / Only on the wall.* Divorce was a psychic break that took years to get over but I never cried for my ex-husband. I haven't missed him for a second. My parents sent my sister to check on me the summer of my separation because everyone thought I was a little too fine, that I must've lost my mind. This other man, who only had tea in my apartment once, I cry about some Sunday nights. Not from sadness, from a fullness that I know may never reach him and settles back onto me instead. I think every Black girl gets a greenhouse in another plane. If we're very lucky, we catch glimpses of it, then visit it at will. If we're even luckier, one or two people dwell inside with us, for a time or forever.

After divorcing, and after I asked this man to exit my garden, I spent two years alone. It didn't occur to me to date. I went to the club wearing cardigans. I went to many Chicago lounges dancing alone, leaving alone. A bass line and my heartbeat: dancing until a melding point, sleeping with ears that felt waterlogged, body still pulsing. Then one evening, my glasses broke in my hands. This recalled an arc deep into *Family Matters'* sixth season: Steve Urkel, an unrepentant geek, creates a DNA-altering substance called "Cool Juice" so he can woo his "African violet": his very vocally disinterested neighbor, Laura Winslow. He gets into a chamber and violently transforms into Stefan Urquelle, who doesn't need glasses. Stefan is smooth and wears suits. Laura immediately swoons, and nobody cares Steve is gone. When my glasses came apart like a prop, I threw them away and carried on with my moderately poor vision. At a friend's gallery opening, I was approached by hot people of all genders and aesthetics, at first looking over my shoulder and moving when they made eyes at me, sure that I was in the way. As a dramatic geek with Urkel tendencies, I stumbled out of the event, unsure what had changed so quickly. I leaned against a brick wall and called my sister: *They're throwing their panties at me! What do I do?* My sister laughed and said to catch them, or just go home. I walked to a train station and under that full moon, a new figure broke loose.

For most of the next decade, I flirted and dated recklessly. There were dalliances and mind games and dead-end relationships. I'd recognized my softness in my garden but it'd take years and a lot of therapy to disrupt patterns, change perspectives, and stop testing my tender flesh. *Your heart isn't open to me,* said one ex, then another. I always had an excuse. Well, he's having studio visits at eleven p.m. in his apartment like he's Biggie Smalls and this is a VH1 special. I'm not Faith Evans, I'm Lil' Kim. No man claims me, neither do I claim one. In the absence of ice that blings, ice of gaze and sentiment. I'm not sure what the final fights were about anymore but I remember men ruining my meals: a taco bowl, a side of lamb, a spring-onion risotto. As a student, I'd found an article tucked in a copy of Uno Chiyo's biography. She'd cry over men for three days, then put on a new kimono and go outside. My breakup dresses are hanging in the closet now, dry-cleaned and ready to menace, though my breasts and hips, and heart and stomach, have changed.

From time to time, I remember my beloved's eyes on me, how they were unchanging, regardless of our moods, what I was wearing, where we were, or who was watching. On an afternoon in 2013 while waiting for brunch at Pearl's, I gave myself to Chaka Khan's "I'm Every Woman," feeling, for the first time, that I could evolve into a woman who's also a spell. I briefly opened my eyes to see him watching me with awe, in the biblical sense. He was seeing a remarkable woman. So he remarked upon me: *Wow,* he breathed before our last meal together, which was also his first word when we'd met in an office corridor years before. He didn't stop looking, and I wasn't shy of him and so kept singing and swaying. My fear of seeking a similar gaze haunts me, as does the fact that I stayed with people whose eyes revealed contempt. *Grow up,* they'd say. *Stop daydreaming. We're not teenagers anymore.* I let them try to break my greenhouse glass, let ferns wilt but not die. I left. I started again. I left again.

Dating is strange because most people won't admit they're dealing with ghosts, echoes, or both. They're facing you, speaking to an ex. Then your reply is lost because they're stuck in an old conversation laced with old hurts, insults you never spoke. I remember an incensed boyfriend kept insisting that I'd called him "cruel." I'd never called anyone cruel. It wasn't part of my fight vocabulary because I'm not one of the Brontë sisters. It turned out his mother had said that to him as a child, which is a whole separate issue. Don't date mama's boys. It's always a dusty Mary-and-Jesus dynamic except both parties often lack righteous attributes.

Sometimes there are two people with two or more ghosts present. Sometimes two silent people think they're talking but it's the sound of ricochets and hard falls. Then there are the cinematic acts of memory and fantasy, the projections with no known operator, the well-worn and familiar scripts ready to perform: bypassing vulnerable, unrehearsed dialogue and taking shortcuts to summarize who someone is. The movie plays at 2x speed so you don't look too hard, listen too closely, get too hurt. The hard work of watching a figure made in your image, the accuracies and offenses mingling into a blur of persona. It shouldn't have surprised me that the scripts for Black women were suffocating. *Who here will leap past problems of imagination?* I found no one ready, including myself. No matter. I had an eternity to tend to my greenhouse.

I'd always been comfortable going to dinners, films, concerts, banquets, beaches, by myself. A stranger offers their idea of consolation: *A woman like you, alone? What has the world come to!* When the pandemic began in 2020, I felt skin hunger for the first time: a nervous, urgent need to be covered and held tight. And the vacuum-like absence of electricity generated by another presence. I witnessed the breakdown of community, the revelation that I and many others had centered biological family and the erotic-romantic. In this era of widespread illness and environmental calamity, I reconsidered the Romantics. John Keats, dying of tuberculosis, aiming to retether himself to the earth and to his senses. A self-involved practice made divine because it was seeking the All. My ex-husband used to cite Keats and say, *Haha, pathetic fallacy*, whenever it rained but he appeared to be in a good mood. Perhaps those were confessions. Then again, he fought with me for days, claiming that the phrase was "nip it in the butt" and not "bud." When people ask what went wrong, I use an African shorthand: *He don't know how to talk to people.*

To pretend COVID hasn't marked breath, touch, sex, and who sleeps in your house is killing hearts, especially in New York City, where we slept to the hum of refrigerated trucks or watched people address a trailer from a distance, flowers in hand, unable to touch the metal housing such precious cargo. I tell partnered friends riding out a rough patch to get all the way back in the house and draw their curtains. The streets today are indescribable. Meet-cutes that result in relationships or seasonal flings were a fever dream. Now we have circular text conversations, something called a "situationship" that I'm too old to investigate, and dating apps. Oh, the disruptive culture of swiping past hundreds of faces. A few weeks in, I found myself mentally swiping people I passed on the sidewalk and quit apps for months. Anyway, no one appreciated my corny jokes. I told a NASA guy he was GO for staging, looking up the Apollo 11 transcript to get the lingo right. *Ok Cindy Crawford*, I messaged a man with a distinctive mole. A lawyer asked to move the conversation to our phones and I replied: *Motion to dismiss (Hinge chat)*. There are signals of anti-Blackness, transphobia, fatphobia, slut-shaming, baked into people's bios. There are very tall men wanting me for chiropractic reasons. There are average-size men wanting me for their Build-a-LeBron workshop. The general headassery can eventually pierce the softest lovers: who says hi first, the silences, the questionnaires, the catfish accusations (my reply always being: *Mm, catfish and greens and mac and cornbread*).

I know I'm part of the problem. Half the time, I want to offer daters free portraits because it's obvious a performance of beauty and personality is unfamiliar. Gear, angles—photographer friends give some of us a ridiculous advantage. In my defense, the pickings are reprehensible. This Frankenstein bio captures at least 90 percent of men seeking women in NYC: *You can find me faster here: IG choco-loco389 [chocolate bar emoji]. Nobody reads this [yawn emoji]. Maybe if you females actually TALK [eye-roll emoji]. Be nice but dirty [devil emoji; googly-eye with tongue out emoji]. Let's skip the small talk [smirk emoji].* Men in Black *is a documentary [alien emoji]. No drama please [light-skinned yogi emoji]. Will probably like your dog better than you [puppy emoji; wink emoji]. My mom says I'm handsome [a photo with his mom that has weird vibes]. If you don't like my dog, I'll kill you. No witches [light-skinned man with arms crossed emoji].*

I once calculated my match-back rate as less than 1 percent. I ran out of people on three different apps. Am I unreasonable? I don't want to date money guys, police and military, or anesthesiologists (what if they get mad at you, and you wake up with your eyebrows reversed?). I wish someone would sue for free race filters because what am I supposed to do with a Thor lookalike named Magnus? Additionally, I'm suspicious there are so many single trainers and fire-fighters. My wax lady who quit dentistry says they're all masochists, and I can't shake her ruling. I don't enjoy fandoms and when people make TV shows their personality. I don't understand why you'd lead a profile stating a food you hate, as if dates are game shows where you're force-fed cilantro or avocado. Also, why is your lactose intol-erance my problem? I'm a lactose supertolerant pastoral African whose grocery cart makes the whites shudder. Why did you list your blood type? If you don't have golden blood, it's not special enough to mention. Why are you sharing makeup preferences if you're not Pat McGrath? If you want fake lashes, just get some, damn! Why are you listing everything you don't want . . . Oh. I see what's happening here. One would think the ghosting and boomeranging, lackluster flirtations, and distinct disinterest in going out would've sent me over the edge. It was a response to a prompt that sat me down for days. *I go crazy for: "Torn" by Natalie Imbruglia.* It can't be, I said in a daze.

Okay, so what *do* I want? This is impossible for a poet to answer, so I distilled the ineffable into one simple filter: *Does this person's gaze move me?* If I'm swiping with the same mechanic commitment as doing squats, I ask myself a question: *Can I see myself in one of these photos, or taking one of these photos?* It's elimination by friend groups, venues, and landscapes. I *want* to write someone a love letter. I *want* to meet someone who feels green and greening. I want someone who doesn't try to erode my happy associations with love. My availability to possibility isn't despite my difficult experiences but because of them. The heartaches just kept pointing me home. I want more experiences like the rare good connections I've made on random days. There was a widower not ready for anything except a walk and a tea, allowing me to witness one of the first times he changed tenses: *This is my wife's favorite song . . . it* was *her favorite song.* There was the musician who played Tevin Campbell's "Can We Talk" and other classics off a speaker as we walked around Brooklyn. At the end of the night, he told me my scent was a planet with many pools. Hours later, he added: *A planet that has rings.* Before he flew back to Paris, he asked me if there was someone in my garden. *It's okay if there is,* he said. *Every woman is entitled to her secret garden.* That was two years ago, and now ours is a memes-based friendship way more consistent and stable than our short-lived romance. The search is well worth it when people surprise us, open for us, and allow us to open for them.

I want to give myself respite, to locate wounds and finger those scars with the same touch I give my plants when they're straining to live. To center romance for romance's sake: because I am alive, of nature, and so, subject to failure, renewal. When I try to explain my needs through lyric and image, my mom grumbles that she'll never have grandchildren at this rate. If the character count allowed it, my dating profile would be this foundational exchange at Garfield Park Conservatory in 2013: After I left the Islamic school with my single-hood documents in hand, I sat in the Fern Room. The whir of fans, the water nearly noiseless on leaves and rocks, the mechanical gurgle of the mini waterfall. The horticulturalist, a Tanzanian man who'd restored the site after a catastrophic hailstorm, stood nearby with a hose. I asked him if he ever dreamed of this place. He said: *Only on the days I water, because it's all I do, for eight hours or more.* He ended watering days with an hour-long workshop for people with challenged houseplants. *People don't accept when a plant is dying, especially if it's a rare or expensive one,* he said. *They want you to do something. I tell them: Look, there's nothing you can do. Every living thing has its own information, and it tells you when it needs to die.*

Is love a living thing? I sat until closing, until my hair smelled like the soil. *Each thing with its own means to its own ends,* I thought. *The ferns, the moss, the bird grazing the greenhouse ceiling. Every thing knows what to do, how to live. Moves with the water and the light. So why not me?*

The Gorilla

JOSEPH EARL THOMAS

With the gorilla having broken into our apartment, I understood that it was my duty as the eldest son to take care of it. My father, with one forearm squeezed between the gorilla's molars, said, "Here, take this," and tossed me a six-shooter with his off hand. As I failed to catch the weapon, it clanged and then slid across the glass coffee table. Nothing shattered or went off. I picked up the weapon, fumbling with it a little; the hot muzzle burned my inner palm as the oven once had, in my rush to procure fish sticks without a mitten. Then I aimed up at the gorilla's face, close enough to feel its warm breath and mangy fur tickle my skin, and hesitated before firing. The barrel rotated. Clicked and rotated, clicked and rotated, and I kept pulling. Nothing happened. The gorilla glanced at me, hardly grimacing, and continued gnawing my father's arm.

"I'm sorry," my father said. "I've grown so old."

Then the gorilla reached for me, but just as its thick fingers grazed the right sleeve of my yellow Pikachu shirt, Dad elbowed the gorilla in its eye and told me to flee upstairs and try to escape out of my sister's bedroom window. I glanced at the half-open front door before following instructions. He wanted me to hop down off the roof and run to buy a new gun and ammunition. I would take my dad's wallet from the right pocket of his Carhartt jacket and gather the required items as quickly as possible.

I was off. I dashed upstairs and into my sister's room, where she and my younger brother were playing *Mario Kart*. I told them both to stay quiet because Dad was being eaten by a gorilla downstairs and they said okay. Then I popped the screen out of her window and jumped out onto the roof, then down into the street, spraining my ankle. It was warm out. A perfect day for a gorilla attack, and I felt guilty that I had not prepared better for the inevitable. Dad had always told me this would happen but I'd slacked off instead, doing kid things: playing *Mario Kart* and masturbating with lotion, making fish sticks for dinner instead of beef-flavored pot pie, and crying.

Rushing down Frankford Avenue, I ran into the pawnshop next to where I got my hair cut every other Friday and knocked against the glass.

"Hey!" I said. "Hey! I need a gun quick!"

"Young man," the clerk said, "for what do you need a gun so quickly?"

"My father," I said, "my American father," running out of breath and gesticulating wildly. "In trouble. Gorilla. Eat him."

"Young man," the clerk said, "gorillas don't eat people. You're being silly." Then he rubbed his chin for a second. "Do you have ID?"

And despite having grabbed my father's wallet, I'd forgotten my own. *Shit.* "No, sir," I said. "But I can bring it back after, please, I just need the gun now."

"No ID, no gun," the clerk said. "Best I can offer you is a hunting rifle, or a shotgun."

But the rifle and shotgun were too heavy; they took up too much space in my inventory. I burst out of the store sweating, thinking more quickly than each of my feet could hit the ground and having no idea where I was running to. I began calculating how long it would take to go back home, grab my ID, and then get a new gun and ammunition from the pawnshop. How long would it take a gorilla to fully eat a two-hundred-and-fifty-pound mostly muscle person? At what point in the mastication process would my father be hurt most? The physics of fending off the gorilla invaded my head, a death clock ticking over Dad's oozing arm. How long could he make it without me? And what was worse, how would I face him were I to come home empty-handed? The disappointment might kill us both. I'd be letting down my brother and sister too, who I'd known since their adoptions needed me to protect them. How would I even get back into the house if the gorilla chewing up Dad's arm decided to block the way? By now the neighbors had probably shown up to watch, as we often did during a gorilla attack. My running through them into the house, over Dad's chewed-up arm too, would interrupt the whole sequence; I'd make everything more difficult. Already, everything was more difficult.

But then someone off the street grabbed my arm. It was T. J.

"Yo, little man," he said. "Where you runnin so fast?"

"It's my father, T. J. He needs my help. There's a gorilla. I need a gun, but I forgot my ID. Just let me go, man!"

"Why you talkin like that?"

"Like what?" I said.

"Never mind." T. J. shook his head. "How much you tryna spend?" He was smiling now. "If I don't got it, I can get it for you," he said.

"I need it now!" is what came out of my mouth in a rush. I raised my voice a little too much, so that it cracked and my ears got hot.

"Aye, calm the fuck down, little man," T. J. said. "I don't wanna have to slap you." Then he took a knee and opened up his black Jan-Sport with *Dragon Ball Z* characters graffitied on it. "Look at these."

T. J.'s wares were impressive: a Colt 45; two Berettas, one silver and one black; a blunderbuss that looked like it was made for killing werewolves; an AK-47; three collapsed AR-15s; a used M16 and two M4s; and a purple Desert Eagle with pink tassels hanging from the grip, same as the handlebars on my little sister's bike. Watching my eyes linger on this last item, T. J. said, "Not that one, shorty. That's mine."

"Okay, T. J. I want the blunderbuss and the silver Beretta," I said. "How much?"

"Damn, young boul, you mean business, huh?"

"It's a gorilla, T. J. Gorillas mean business. I need to help my father and—"

"Can you please stop fuckin talkin like that," he said. "I need you to stop fuckin talkin like that before I slap the shit outta you." Then he paused for a moment while I sweated it out in the heat. "How much you got, man?"

I rifled through my dad's wallet. "Like five hundred," I said.

"Okay," T. J. replied. "You can gimme that, but you owe me."

"Fine. Whatever you want. I need to help my family."

And with that, I handed all of Dad's cash over to T. J. and grabbed both of the guns. Right after which T. J. slithered into an alley, touching two fingers to his eyes and pointing them at mine like, I see you. I sprinted in the direction of home, until a sinking feeling hit me; I had forgotten about ammunition. But I still had my dad's credit cards and wallet, so I ran off toward the nearest Target superstore, which turned out to be not that super since they did not have ammunition or cigarettes, which I anticipated my father would want after the ordeal. On my way out, an older woman pushing a walker suggested I try Walmart a few blocks down.

I arrived in such a hurry that I couldn't even explain what I needed, I just threw the guns down on the table in the sporting goods section and, while praising them for their cleanness and how well-maintained they were, the man at the counter, chewing dip, laid down a big box of ammunition. It was on sale, rolled back from seventeen ninety-nine a box to three dollars and fifty cents per box. This was exciting because I knew Dad would be glad I found such a deal. When I withdrew a credit card, the man informed me that I would need to purchase at least ten dollars' worth of merchandise in order to use credit or debit, so I bought four boxes. Two for the blunderbuss and two for the Beretta. Then the chip reader wasn't working, so I had to swipe the card several times, which worried me, despite the salesman saying there would be no additional charges. Waiting for the receipt to print, I suddenly realized I had to pee, and was bouncing up and down. Running again helped calm my bladder; I was on the street again in an instant, guns in hand, pulling ammo out of my plastic bag and loading the weapons without losing stride. I dropped things, but that was fine.

The time to end the gorilla was now. From half a block away, I could eye the commotion around our front door, which was by then smashed down. A crowd had gathered: Mrs. Cealy and them, the Michaelsons and their newborn, my most recent crush and their abusive father. And through the crowd, one thick and hairy calf muscle stuck out, moving just enough to imagine the other end of its personage gnawing ever so slowly on human flesh. *Good,* I thought. *This means Dad is still holding the gorilla off.* But when I wormed through the onlookers and stepped through the door I couldn't find Dad at all. And there were two gorillas, not one. They were mid coitus, doggy-style, and the one receiving penetration gazed longingly out of the living room window, its chin knocking against our radiator. I could not distinguish pain from ecstasy as they switched to missionary, but I knew from a previous internet search that other animals also had sex for pleasure. The neighbors were silent amid the grunting and knocking of the gorillas. My siblings had come halfway down the stairs, now sitting with a big bag of plain potato chips. They were the only ones to meet my gaze when I entered. Both gorillas ignored me, and I was able to draw my new blunderbuss and, inches from the top of the first gorilla's head, pull the trigger. The weight of the blast hurt my wrist and shoulder, rippled through my chest. After the explosion there was a splashing sound, as the inner materials of gorilla life made contact with walls, curtains, and the faces of spectators.

To my surprise, the second gorilla hardly seemed to notice. It turned back over on all fours with urgency, and continued gesticulating in the same manner, pushing up against nothing but air after the first body fell. I looked around the room, saddened by the knowledge that I would later have to clean all of this up.

Finally, as I was reloading, the second gorilla looked up at me, still moving its butt as if it would always be on the receiving end of another's sexual satisfaction, whether the other was present or not. It seemed less startled than disappointed, like it knew I was making a mistake but could offer no other resolution to the situation in which we found ourselves. I repeated the act with regard to the second gorilla and even lying on the floor, near headless, it flexed its body a few more times. The neighbors, seeing all they'd needed to see, dispersed. My siblings went back upstairs to play their game.

I yelled and yelled for my father, scrambling around the house, but there was no sign of him anywhere, so I grabbed a knife from the kitchen. With some effort I rolled the first gorilla over on its back, exposing the abdomen so that I could begin carving. Working my wrist so as not to cut too deeply, I cut in a large circle around the farthest-protruding sections of the animal, not too deeply, but far enough through the thick hide to gain access to its insides. By the time my back began hurting, I ended up with an oval pattern of excised flesh. From inside, just beneath a thick layer of viscera, I could hear muffled sounds. My siblings, either hearing the sounds as well or just out of sheer curiosity, came back halfway down the stairs.

"Eldest brother, what are you doing?" they said.

"I'm just lookin for Dad," I said. "Y'all go upstairs and play. I'll come get you in a minute."

"Okay," they replied in unison, frolicking back up the stairs.

Then I started to dig. The fatigue, from all the running and carrying and digging, made me sad, I think, or made me realize I'd been sad for quite some time with little time to think about it. But a trace of my father vanquished this thought; I could feel him, human skin and bone tangled in gorilla small intestine, folded over a bulky liver and yet, reaching out to me. I wanted to wipe my face but was afraid of disease transmission from all the gorilla interior, thinking about how they're so close to us, and also, the way our cat had died from Feline Immunodeficiency Virus and Dad had warned us not to share food with it lest we contract cat AIDS. I shut my eyes tight in order to feel better and kept carving. It was a new knife, still sharp and hardly used; I'd bought it as a Father's Day gift a long time ago, but soon after, Dad had stopped cooking altogether. I considered this as I kept carving, putting the knife to good use. Everything had a use it could be put to. It just needed a body to do the putting. Soaked in warm slush now, and drawing the small intestine over my shoulder, I wondered how surgeons kept so clean on television. The gorilla parts were heavy. Heaving them to the side with a deep splosh onto the hardwood floor, I slowed down to catch my breath before digging in to displace the gorilla's hips and crack ribs open until there was nothing left but softness. And deep from within the cavern of gorilla, I felt my father's hand grasp mine tight; I could sense the contours of his face, his cheeks dimpled into a hard smile.

"Dad, I did it!" I told him. "I did it!"

Then he loosened his hand from mine, big and warm as it was, before churning it into that classic thumbs-up he'd given me when I learned to tie my shoelaces as a child, which I had hardly seen since I was a child, letting me know, at long last, that I was good and ready, and that he was so proud, finally proud enough to rest.

From: Emily ▓▓▓▓▓▓▓▓▓▓▓▓▓▓
To: Damon Young ▓▓▓▓▓▓▓▓▓▓▓▓▓▓
Subject: Racism Is Really Bad

I just read "Racism Is Really Bad" and I'm so fucking tired of white people and being a white person. We are so fucking awful. I hate myself. I hate my white skin and my even-whiter-than-my-white-skin teeth. I hate milk, white sheets of paper, Wite-Out, white chalk, white plaster, white turkey meat, ranch dressing, fettuccine Alfredo, polar bears, saltshakers, Mentos, iPhone chargers, Norway, and Nicole Kidman. I can't even eat popcorn or play the piano anymore, because the whiteness on the kernels and the keys infuriates me. Sometimes I look in the mirror in the morning and I just want to peel my skin off like an orange, taking each layer of whiteness off and tossing it in the trash with the rest of the fucking garbage. Actually, since oranges are covered in white pith after you peel them, that analogy doesn't quite work. I guess bananas and apples and pears don't either. Shit, have you ever realized how disgustingly white most fruit is when you peel the outer layers off? Goddamn, there's no end to this shit.

   Fuck racism, fuck white people, fuck whiteness, and fuck fruit.

Emily

The Jackie Robinson Society

*

WYATT CENAC

Thank you. It's truly an honor to be speaking today in front of all of you, the newest inductees into the Jackie Robinson Society for Negroes Foolish Enough to Be the First to Do Anything Around White People. Among you sits the first Black student body president at a predominantly white high school in Seattle. Congrats. Just know they are coming. If you get a C on a math test, they will try to impeach you!

I see the first Black woman puppeteer on *Sesame Street*. So proud. Keep an eye on Oscar the Grouch, he's got . . . opinions. A few rows back, I see the first Black attorney to make partner at a prestigious Philadelphia law firm. Save every email. Forward it to a nonwork account. Document everything, bro. You might have to sue them later. And down in front, I see the first Black fry cook ever at the Winston-Salem Hardee's location number 431. Why did it take so long? Because the manager didn't trust Black folks near the oil. And today, look who's making french fries. It's Keisha!

But it's that type of white nonsense—the requests to touch your hair. It's the memes passed around on the company Slack channel that your coworker "didn't realize were offensive." And all of the fist bumps. So many fist bumps that you will have to endure when a handshake would have sufficed. Looking around this secret banquet hall beneath the Magic Johnson's TGI Fridays, I see the brave Black souls who dared to be the canaries in the coal mines of white people's ignorance.

Today, you join the ranks of great Jackie Robinson Society members such as Barack Obama and Mae Jemison, the first Black woman to go to outer space. Why did she come back? She knows what it's like down here. She couldn't have planted a flag on the moon and renamed it for Marcus Garvey? Or . . . was space worse?

There are members like Thomas L. Jennings, the first Black person to hold a patent. He invented dry cleaning. Other Black people had invented things before him, but Thomas Jennings was the first one whom a white guy decided not to pretend to give a patent to and then steal that Black excellence for himself. There's Ethel Waters, the first Black person to star in a TV show. Gotta wonder how often a cameraman thought she was part of the catering crew? Answer: every damned day!

Speaking of catered meals, I'm reminded of Jackie Robinson Society member Booker T. Washington, who holds the distinction of being the first Black person invited to *eat* at the White House. Black folks might have built the place and worked inside it, but he was the first Negro to be allowed to eat. All those other Black folks just had to stay hungry. *Black folks might have been making Thomas Jefferson's mac and cheese, but he was not letting them taste it.* Booker T. had to sit there as Teddy Roosevelt probably explained to him what a fork does. And Booker T. quietly nodded, while on the inside wanting to stab that man in the forehead for that patronizing white foolishness; but Booker T. knew that in Teddy's fork-punctured mind, his point would have been proven.

The list of esteemed Jackie Robinson Society for Negroes Foolish Enough to Be the First to Do Anything Around White People members is long. There's Beyoncé Knowles, who was the first Black woman to headline Coachella. Might not seem like much, but she had to keep her composure as a sea of white faces too-proudly sang, *You mix that Negro with that Creole, get a Texas Bama!* Which from her voice sounds great, but from theirs . . . like the studio audience for a game show about plantation eugenics called *Who Wants to Build a Slave.*

And obviously, there's the man for whom this society is named, Mr. Jackie Robinson himself. And to be clear, this society has existed since long before Jackie Robinson showed up to work one day and thought, *Welp, this job is about to get passive-aggressive.* But since that day in 1947 when he suited up for the Brooklyn Dodgers and became the league's first Black player, Jackie Robinson has become synonymous with being the first to endure being in an all-white space. The man's name is damn near a verb for integration! I mean, what if I told you Jackie Robinson wasn't even the first Black person to play Major League Baseball. It was a guy named Moses Walker. He Jackie Robinsoned Jackie Robinson!

But Major League Baseball celebrates Jackie Robinson Day because it's better than celebrating Moses Walker Day as the day a Black man broke the color barrier and white folks got mad, ran him out, and decided to rebuild that barrier for another sixty-plus years. As an aside, "breaking the color barrier" makes it sound like Jackie Robinson did some magic trick where he broke out of a giant egg and solved racism. If he did that, it would have been pretty cool, possibly gooey, and probably a lot less exhausting than what he really had to do, which was be great at baseball while having to carry a shit-ton of racism by himself as a bunch of white people used his name to take a victory lap and say, "Hey, we're a little less racist," while still being pretty damned racist. Jackie Robinson Day is for them, the Jackie Robinson Society is for us.

Many years ago, I got my first real job and induction into this fine society. See, I became the first Black writer or person hired on a show that had been around for almost a decade. It took them seven years to hire a Black person and it only happened because there had been a public outcry at the lack of diversity in Hollywood. Now, you'd think if somebody came to your TV show and said, "Hey, don't you think it's a little weird that you seem to only be hiring white dudes?" that might be embarrassing enough to get introspective, take responsibility, and be proactive. But who wants to do that? Not a lot of white dudes in New Balance sneakers and Dockers flat-front slacks.

Instead, the TV studios had to incentivize the TV shows to hire minorities, by saying if a show could simply hire one person of color, then the studio would pay that writer's salary instead of it going against the show's budget. And even then, many television shows were still dragging their feet despite being offered a *free writer* . . . which is the term the white head writer used to refer to me when I became the first Black writer in that TV writers' room.

This white dude relished the fact that I was "free." He would bring it up often, reminding me that I was a "bonus writer" because I cost the show nothing. Perhaps he thought by saying it so many times, he was letting me know that I was a gift to the show, but a white guy crowing about how he's getting "free labor" from a Black person feels like something to go to HR about . . . if there had been a person of color in HR . . . or even an HR department. For him, I was some kind of coupon for racial progress that also added much-needed speed to the lineup of the office softball team. Although, unlike Jackie Robinson, I couldn't play first base for shit.

After every slight or annoyance, I would return to the Jackie Robinson Society. This underground bunker with its faint scent of mozzarella sticks and a surplus of stolen Lakers office supplies became a safe space for me. Hearing the stories of fellow inductees, I felt less alone at my job even though I was. As I said, this was my first real job. I didn't want this white man's ignorance to fuck it up for me. Because that's what it'd do. He'd be fine either way, but this was an opportunity that could lay a foundation for my career. And while it did, it also laid a foundation for what it would be like to navigate white spaces even with people who consider themselves allies.

You can get inducted into the Jackie Robinson Society for multiple things. I was, thanks to another boss who, before hiring me, proudly joked about the lack of diversity he employed while receiving an Emmy Award. A few years later, I guess I became his award for first Black person he felt like hiring. Having membership in the Jackie Robinson Society for Negroes Foolish Enough to Be the First to Do Anything Around White People was invaluable the day I learned that while I was away from the office, this white man engaged in a debate with a bunch of other white people about who could say the word "nigger," while happily saying the word! My guess is that was a conversation he wouldn't have been as comfortable having had I been in the room that day, but what was clear was that having my presence in the office was enough for him to feel like he'd done the work.

You inductees probably already know, when you're the first Black person at any job, you'll quickly learn that white fragility is more than a book. It's the cream in every cup of their morning coffee. One of these bosses once did a voice that I found a bit racially offensive. Now, since he wasn't Black, one might think he'd defer to the sole Black employee saying "This bothers me" and perhaps respond with something like, "I'm sorry. I should try to understand where you're coming from." Instead, the dude screamed "fuck off," repeatedly and loudly enough for everyone in the office to hear. If there had been an HR department, maybe there would have been somebody in the building whom I could have turned to in that moment for guidance or even support. Instead, I found myself back here, under La Tijera Boulevard in the Cross Colours Lounge of the JRS, trading stories with Eric Holder and the ghost of Althea Gibson about how that boss never actually apologized for screaming at an employee like a petulant child . . . unless you count him offering me a fist bump.

There was another job where, while filming a scene for a television show, a random stranger drove by shouting "nigger" and the entire crew turned and looked at me. Were they looking at me to see how I might react or were they looking because I was the only person around who fit the bill? And while they all told me how horrible that moment was for them, they never seemed to mind the fact that there were crew members with tattoos of the Confederate flag.

Or the job that took me into a neo-Nazi's home, where I became the first Black man to sit on a white supremacist's Raymour & Flanigan sofa. And as uncomfortable as I was with the idea of being in the home of a man criminally convicted of racist acts, the only white coworker who seemed to agree with me at the time was a dude who, years later, would get arrested for taking part in the *Capitol Riot, Insurrection, and Holiday Spectacular,* which goes to show that white allyship can turn on a dime.

And I share that with all of you, as you sit here in your Jackie Robinson Society velvet jackets and matching sweatpants, because there is no trophy for being the first Black person in a white space. It pains me to say, but we are the trophy. For them.

What you accomplished is impressive. Your achievement is worthy of praise, recognition, and celebration. But they won't do it, which is why the Jackie Robinson Society for Negroes Foolish Enough to Be the First to Do Anything Around White People exists. While I'm sure we all wish we could live in a world where there weren't so many, many things that white people have actively shut us out of, you should all be proud of what you've each done. I'm proud of you. You pushed through a door that their ignorance was okay closing off to you and so many before you.

Look, being a fry cook is not the same as being the president of the United States, but when you're the first Black person to do it, chances are you may have to employ some of the same skills in diplomacy and possibly border security of the personal kind. I'm sure Barack Obama had to tell a few people not to call him "boy" or "son." And you probably will too, Keisha. Because even though we celebrate these accomplishments, we also commiserate over the things we've had to endure. From blaccents to dumb comments to outright racist behavior, these aren't microaggressions or macroaggressions. They are all just bullshit that you don't deserve.

And while we wait for Mae Jemison to get off her butt and build the Black Star Rocket Ship that can take us all to a planet free from white nonsense, we have the Jackie Robinson Society for Negroes Foolish Enough to Be the First to Do Anything Around White People so that we can be there for one another. Where we can share a knowing nod and even laugh at the frustrating, maddening, and downright dumb things we've had to put up with while white people "figure out" some shit we already knew.

An Oral History of the Holy Ghost

✳

MICHAEL HARRIOT

Giving honor to Jesus, Damon Young, the saints of God, and all the members of this book's pulpit. Before I begin, I think it is necessary to list the qualifications that make me one of America's foremost experts on the Black Holy Ghost.

I did not descend from kings and queens. My ancestors were shit-starters. Rabble-rousers. Troublemakers. Instead of being blessed with social status and verbal self-restraint, the Harriot Clan was selected to beta-test an early version of the Holy Ghost specifically developed for African America.

The tale dates back to James Bradley, a wealthy South Carolina businessman who discovered that his enslaved servant Earvin could read and write. Because of Earvin's considerable skills as a blacksmith, James overlooked Earvin's illegal literacy and smart mouth, even allowing him to preach on plantations in the Salem district of South Carolina. Before Bradley died, he filed his will at the local courthouse, dividing more than two hundred slaves between his six children. To save his progeny the trouble of dealing with human chattel as cunning and rebellious as Earvin, Bradley ignored South Carolina's proclamation against manumission and issued one final set of instructions for the executors of his estate.

"My belligerous Negro Man Earvin is to have his own time," reads

Bradley's 1849 will. "He is not to be appraised when my estate is valued and no further service is required of him."

Even though he was destitute and homeless, Earvin had three valuable possessions that would provide his descendants with generational wealth: his smart mouth, blacksmithing skills, and the Holy Ghost.

A century later, Earvin's great-granddaughter Marvell Bradley became the first Black woman to work at Sonoco, a global paper company a few miles from James Bradley's forced-labor farm. There, she met and married James Harriot, a machinist and third-generation Holy Ghoster. They purchased a small parcel of land, and in 1956, James and Marvell finished building the cinder-block house that would become my childhood home. As soon as they finished, they began holding church services in that dwelling, founding the congregation that evolved into the Household of Faith Holiness Church, Pillar and Ground of Truth, House of Prayer for All People.* The Household of Faith eventually built its own sanctuary, but it still serves as the Harriot family's Holy Ghost headquarters.

HOF was also the center of my preadult life. It was basically Holy Ghost Hogwarts—a magnet school for people who have "the anointing." And because I was homeschooled and raised by a literal church family, I've had very little non–Holy Ghost influence in my early life. I'm basically a Holy Ghost prodigy.

Despite my lifelong education in this real-life caricature of the proverbial "Black Church,"† I have no actual firsthand experience with the Holy Ghost. Don't get me wrong. I desperately *wanted* the Holy Ghost—if only to see what it was like to be struck by Jesus's lightning and faint from an overwhelming need to Harlem Shake to organist accompaniment. But alas, I have never even shed a tear during a prayer circle. While this revelation may cause you to immediately dismiss my wealth of knowledge, I would argue that more than forty years of being draped in prayers, dabbed with anointing oils, and cov-

---

* Yes, that is the actual name, which was shortened to "Church #3" because the Hartsville chapter was the third of seven Household of Faiths sprinkled across South Carolina.
† Not *a Black Church*, but "the Black Church"—the collective religious institution of Black America.

ered by God's grace has imbued me with as deep an understanding of the Holy Ghost as anyone who ever walked the face of the earth.

To be fair, it is impossible to *fully* understand the Holy Ghost. This may seem contradictory but there are a lot of things we accept without truly understanding them. I don't know why planes don't get wet when they fly through clouds. If fish drink water, why hasn't the ocean turned to pee? I took AP physics and still don't really know what the fuck gravity is. And when it comes to the Holy Ghost, there are certain things you have to accept on faith.

First, you need to understand that this cultural phenomenon is not the same thing as the Holy Spirit. In churches where choirs sound like human bagpipes, the Holy Spirit is part of a three-man executive suite known as the "Holy Trinity" that includes the original single Father and his Son. "Spirit" is something that cheerleaders have and heathens drink, while "Ghosts" are invisible souls of ancestors. You can kill someone's spirit, but aside from one member of the Wu-Tang Clan, you can't murder a ghost.* Black people aren't afraid of spirits but we don't fuck with ghosts.

The Black Holy Ghost is a pure, uncut form of Christianity that reveals itself in two different ways. The most common version is the "catchable" Holy Ghost—when God's essence becomes so radioactively contagious that it spontaneously combusts in the feet of churchgoers during praise and/or worship. When one "catches" the Holy Ghost, they may begin shouting in the form of a ritual dance that resembles a cross between Crip Walking and a Que Dog stepping to "Atomic Dog."†

The second kind of Holy Ghost is a more permanent version that can only be acquired during the last phase of the following three-step ritual:

1. **Saved:** After accepting Black Jesus as your Lord and Savior, you dress in flowing white clothes and allow a registered Holy Ghost authority to dip you in God's dunk tank.

---

* Even he is limited to killing a ghost's face.
† This is the origin of most African American dance steps, including the Charleston, the running man, and the Diddy Dance. In fact, most fraternity step routines are just nonreligious Holy Ghost shouts set to call-and-responses.

2. **Sanctified:** You purge your life of bad things like drinking alcohol, using the word "motherfucker," and listening to any secular music that inspires involuntary hip movement.
3. **Filled with the Holy Ghost:** Your prayers receive VIP treatment and a chosen few people develop superpowers.

Although being saved, sanctified, and filled with the Holy Ghost is like Jesus's version of Amazon Prime, one cannot simply subscribe to the service and receive expedited delivery of God's grace. You have to be "called" by the omnipotent savior himself. Or, in the case of the Harriots, you can simply be born in the line of succession for the family's Holy Ghost privilege.

In 1972, James Harriot passed away, leaving my grandmother as the family's most powerful Holy Ghost practitioner. My grandmother had the Holy Ghost's platinum package, which came with supernatural abilities. She probably could've taken Storm's spot with the X-Men if the professor had known about her. I've seen my grandma extinguish a grease fire by praying over the Holy Ghost pot. Sure, she could've used a fifty-cent box of baking soda, but you don't need an Arm or a Hammer when you have God on your side. Plus, someone with a "carnal mind" might have thought she was cooking crack.

My mother was next in line. She was a rebellious sort who initially rejected her legacy to join the Black Power movement, and in her late teens, she was blinded by a hereditary eye disease that doctors concluded could only be cured by a transplant. Unfortunately, finding a compatible donor in a small town was as likely as a wealthy enslaver freeing his most valuable piece of property. Fortunately, my grandmother had the Holy Ghost.

By the time my mother turned nineteen, she was the recipient of two factory-refurbished eyes, a miracle that demanded she assume her place as the family's head Holy Ghost practitioner. And everyone assumed I, as the person who loved my grandmother and mother more than life itself, was the rightful inheritor of the Harriot Holy Ghost Throne.

I was born by the river, in a little tent.

No, seriously. Because I was afflicted with neonatal seizures and diagnosed with childhood epilepsy, I spent the first few days of my life in an oxygen tent at Byerly Hospital, a stone's throw from an outlet of the Pee Dee River. Luckily, Sister Wilene Jackson, the head usher from the Household of Faith, worked in the newborn intensive care unit as a nurse.

I cannot verify the next part of the story, but here is the legend I was told.

A week after I was born, a few Windsor-knot-wearing men and candy-lady-looking women began gathering in the hospital lobby. Then more came. Then more. Apparently, they had received the Holy Ghost Bat Signal from my grandmother, and before long, Holy Ghost specialists of the highest order filled the waiting room. These prayer warriors were not exclusively from my church. They were the elders and first ladies of Household of Faiths from across the state. They were pastors and prophetesses from congregations around town. The Holy Ghost Avengers had come to save me.

Sister Wilene told them they could not all come into the NICU, and the staff couldn't bring me to the lobby. However, because she was aware of the Super Saiyan saints assembled in that hospital, she reportedly did the next best thing—she brought down the medicine that was supposed to be administered to baby Mikey intravenously. The league of extraordinary Christians formed a prayer circle around the IV bag and began to call upon His holy name. A few days later, I was released from the hospital and told that I would have to take epilepsy drugs for the rest of my life. I would tell you the specific name of the medication, but I have never swallowed a tablet of antiseizure medicine.

I have also never had another seizure.

After Jesus's superfriends *prayed the medicine into my body,* it was only natural to assume that I was gonna be America's Next Top Apostle. However, my miraculous recovery from juvenile myoclonic epilepsy was accompanied by a rare case of early-onset Holy Ghost resistance syndrome. Man, I tried everything to get the Holy Ghost! I kept my eyes closed during Deacon Stevenson's long benediction. I led the prayers in peewee football. I stood in line for every altar call. At the tender age of eight, after signing up for the sick and shut-in list for twenty-seven consecutive weeks, I was summoned to a meeting with the church secretary, the assistant pastor, and the deacon in charge of blessings. "Brother Mikey," Sister Patricia explained while peering at her spiral notebook, "if you're not ill or confined to your home, you can't keep putting yourself on the list, understand?"

I did not.

"Is Jesus running low on grace or something?" I asked. "Y'all can't just cockblock my blessings like this! I want an appeal!"

As soon as the sentence left my mouth, I knew "cockblock" was the wrong word to use in the presence of Elder Johnson, who immediately asked the Lord to forgive me.* Looking back, I think this was the moment when I lost my position as a first-round pick in the Holy Ghost draft. And trust me, in my desperation to claim my Holy Ghost legacy, I've examined every nanosecond of my life to see what I did wrong.

When I broke a mirror dunking on my cousin in a game of bedroom basketball at seven years old, I figured seven years of bad luck meant I could still get my inheritance by fifteen. Maybe my Sabbath school teacher Sister Rosa damned me to a life of second-tier spirituality by accusing me of blasphemy during her lesson on the ten plagues of Egypt. I was simply noting that Pharoah actually wanted to let the children of Israel go; it was God who "hardened the heart of Pharoah" so Moses could do more magic tricks.

What? It was in the Bible!

I have even considered that my name may have prevented me from achieving the pinnacle of African American sanctification. Sure, God is omnipotent, but He may have gotten my name mixed up with a Caucasian Michael Harriot. Everyone knows white people can't catch the Holy Ghost.

There are very few peer-reviewed studies on the causes of Caucasian Holy Ghost immunity, so I can't say whether it's genetics or evolution. I suspect Holy Ghost resistance is related to a lack of rhythm, because I've seen ministers of music play shouting songs that shook

---

* To be fair, I had learned the word "cockblock" from my uncle Junior, a Black Panther who was neither saved nor sanctified. To make up for his blessings deficit, he was forced to sell chickens and marijuana.

the sanctuary, and the white visitors still couldn't catch the beat. And, yes, all of the musicians had the anointing; I checked. All I know is white folk can't "catch" the temporary version or qualify for the permanent kind. I've seen the best and brightest worshipmasters fail to penetrate the Caucasoid epidermis with their heavenly pleas. And all of this was corroborated by scientific evidence during the clinical trial of Tony King.

When I turned eleven, my mother agreed that my three sisters and I had sufficient training in the ways of the Holy Ghost. After much consultation with the Most High, she decided to end our homeschooling and signed us up for public school. As soon as I entered this heathen world, I met my first two non-HOF friends—Gregory Prince and Tony King.

Tony was white, unathletic, and *very nerdy,* but he was my plug for *Mad* magazines, which were too profane for the Harriot household. Gregory was also a geek who suffered from sickle cell anemia and asthma. Gregory was one of the few non-HOF kids I knew before I entered the public education system. His daddy cussed and allowed him to listen to what my grandma called "that boompity boomp music." Still, his family would often call upon my grandmother's Holy Ghost powers whenever he had to endure the excruciating pain of a sickle cell crisis. As a sheltered church kid with no social skills, hanging with Greg and Tony was the *only* time I felt "normal."

To ensure that Tony didn't stop me from achieving everlasting life, I was required to bring him to church. He was happy to join me, and Gregory decided to tag along. I didn't want my new friends to endure a marathon church session, so I decided that our Tuesday night service was the perfect time for this friendship ritual.

On Tuesday nights, I fulfilled the community service requirement for my Holy Ghost résumé by serving as the assistant recording technician for the Household of Faith weekly radio broadcast. I figured the combination of music and a short sermon would make Tony eligible for friend status without my being embarrassed. Since the recording was limited to thirty minutes, the format was always the same. The Hartsville Radio Choir sang a song, followed by a solo from Sister Rosa Lee Hunter, a prayer from Brother Jay, a sermon, and the ad for the pastor's exterminating service, followed by the HOF theme song, which concluded the broadcast.

Yes, the Household of Faith had a theme song, and it was *terrible*. Aside from a complete lack of rhyme, the worst thing about our Holy Ghost jingle was that it was written in the vernacular of twelfth-century pilgrims. Oh, it infuriated me no end. In fact, I suspect this anger may have inadvertently foiled my Holy Ghost ambitions. The song's first verse was awful, but I understood why it was so atrocious. It basically just told the listener who we were:

> *We are the church of the living God*
> *Pillar and ground of truth.*
> *House of prayer for all peeeeee-pull,*
> *Commandment keepers are we.*

Every time I sang that first verse, I subconsciously thought: *God, damn that last line!* (Technically, I wasn't cussing in the Lord's house because I wanted him to damn that specific part of the song.) If you're gonna say, "Fuck rhyming in my song," then why not avoid sounding like Quakers and just say, "We are commandment keepers"? But it was the second verse that really irked my soul.

> *We don't drink no wine.*
> *We don't eat no swine.*
> *Keep the commandments of the Lord Our God*
> *Commandment keepers are we!*

I have no idea why the writer was so proud of our commandment-keeping. Not only have you already informed the audience of our devotion to the commandments, but you have also proven that you can rhyme! Yet, once again, you just threw it all away!! Of course, I never voiced this opinion out loud because our church jingle was written, composed, and arranged by someone with the highest Holy Ghost credentials:

My mother.

Tony and Greg's visit to the HOF coincided with another rite of passage in my life. Because Brother Charles, the main recording engineer, was sick, I was in charge of the entire broadcast, which meant I got to wear the sacred headphones. Wearing Brother Charles's headphones was equivalent to being raised in a firehouse, wearing the uniform, and sliding down the pole. When the broadcast began that evening, I was as focused as my attention-deficit brain would allow when, out of the corner of my eye, I saw Tony standing . . .

For the *theme song*.

How could a friend of mine like that song? It must have been his "carnal mind," because Gregory was still sitting. When Elder Johnson called my friends up for altar call at the end of service, I didn't object because Tony *obviously* needed prayer. Plus, they could both serve as control subjects to help me understand why the Holy Ghost had shunned me. At the very least, I figured that getting saved and sanctified at the HOF would cement our friendship, like military buddies who went through boot camp together. We'd forever be basic-training soldiers in the Army of the Lord.

Tony was up first. Elder Johnson warmed up as usual by calling all of God's street names. By the time he put the Killer Kowalski Claw on Tony's forehead, I had figured it was over. I knew he was getting the most potent prayers when Brother Jay, Deacon Stevenson, and Brother George grabbed each other's shoulders to daisy-chain "the spirit" into Tony. I committed a cardinal sin and stole a peek at the moment Tony reached the Holy Ghost's first base.

Nothing. Not even a hallelujah.

So all this time, it wasn't me! Back then, I didn't know about the genetic defect that prevents people of no color from being electrocuted by a bolt from the Almighty. Tony was proof that my being impervious to the Holy Ghost wasn't my fault. Or maybe it was because he had his eyes open. I assumed everyone knows the Lord works in mysterious ways, which is why you have to shut your eyes while He's doing His thing.

Gregory was next. I didn't even bother to close my eyes because Tony had already proven that, like most non–choir members at the HOF, the Holy Ghost didn't attend the Tuesday night service. I totally understood. I wouldn't listen to that song if I didn't have to, either.

Gregory had been to a Black church, so he already had his eyes closed and his arms in the "bless me" position when the deacons began shooting the Holy Ghost through their shoulders to Elder Johnson's vise-grip fingers. He had barely made it through his warm-up "King of Kings, bright and morning star . . ." when Gregory's hands rose in the air and tears squirted from his eyes. Brother Donald, one of the finest improvisational shouting-music composers the world has ever seen, began playing the organ. Sister Wilma went ballistic on the tambourine. Sister Daisy fainted *two times,* and her reserved seat wasn't even on the front pew!

This motherfucker got the Holy Ghost!

I stood there dumbfounded as Gregory did the Christ Shuffle all over the shouting floor. He was even speaking in tongues, which is honors-level Holy Ghost activity! I tried to remain calm, but God knows what was in my heart, so I'm sure He heard the jealousy burst out from my insides. I was betrayed by my best friend.

It be ya own deities.

Even worse, "Gregory Prince Gets Saved" became a landmark episode of the Household of Faith broadcast. The missionary team handed out dubbed Maxell cassette copies to prove that we were truly the House of Prayer for All People. Gregory never became a member of the Household of Faith, but he became a proud member of Jehovah's street team, extolling the virtues of the Holy Ghost.

The next year, the principal informed my mother that I should skip the sixth grade, so I left Gregory and Tony behind and continued my quest to live up to my family heritage at Hartsville Junior High. As the only Black kid in the honors program, I didn't even bother to try to solicit my white classmates for team Jesus. Fortunately, I had a special agent who could help me navigate this new world. Unfortunately, he didn't have the Holy Ghost.

James "Double-O" Bond* grew up in my church, so he didn't have to pass my family's Holy Ghost trial. Brother Jay, Double-O's grandfather, was saved from a life of sin when his World War II army mate, my grandfather, invited him to church. The patriarch of my family's

---

* Yes, that is his real name.

Holy Ghost legacy died before I was born, so, for all intents and purposes, Brother Jay was my granddaddy too. Double-O was two years older than I was, but we were not close friends because I was homeschooled until I skipped a grade.

The balance provided by our lifelong friendship was seemingly ordained by divine providence. I had three sisters; he had three brothers. Both our mothers were women named Dorothy who had the Holy Ghost. He was athletic, charismatic, and a ladies' man; I was none of that. More than anyone, James is the reason I became content with my non–Holy Ghost fate, because James wasn't ashamed to let anyone know he was a proud sinner.

That summer, Double-O and I signed up for a city basketball league where we played for the Hartsville Lakers. He taught me how to gamble during extended Tonk sessions, and I became his designated Spades partner. His mom was more liberal, so he was allowed to watch R-rated movies and even pornography. (HOF, on the other hand, classified any woman in a bathing suit as a "porn star." *Baywatch* and the *My Baby Got Back* series were one and the same.) The evidence of my backsliding became obvious when I started sitting with Double-O in the rear of the church. My May-December friendship with Double-O catapulted me into circles that I could have never infiltrated on my own. I was allowed to hang with high schoolers and was even welcomed into his rap group, El Crew. As I adopted Double-O's do-what-you-want lifestyle, I justified my actions by blaming my heathen ways on Jesus.

If the Good Lord didn't want me to play Spades, then why did He bless me with six and a possible?* If I had the Holy Ghost, maybe I wouldn't have resigned from my telecommunications ministry position to be a basketball team benchwarmer. God made all things, including the big joker, *Beverly Hills Cop,* and the body of every *Jet* magazine Beauty of the Week. If I'm a sinner, then it's really His fault.

After one year of junior high heathenism, James went on to high

---

* In the HOF doctrine, using the Bicycle playing cards for *any game* was a sin. You could play Uno or Trivial Pursuit but Jesus was the only king we acknowledged.

school while I returned to my previous status as an outcast nerd. Even though El Crew still had our after-school writing sessions and basketball practices, I was stuck at school for most of the day with lowly, immature middle schoolers. In the absence of my high school buddies, I was forced to rekindle my relationship with my old crew—Tony and Greg. By day, I was an upstanding citizen who hung with Holy Ghosters who listened to the Mississippi Mass Choir during 4B lunch. On nights and weekends, I was a card-playing B-boy who cussed a little bit. For an entire school year, I lived a double life.

The next year, I left Tony and Greg behind and entered high school. James and I became inseparable. We freestyled while walking to church. We met at each other's houses *before school*. I hung out with James's upperclassman friends during lunch and played basketball and football with them after school. I wasn't even a person anymore; I was part of a duo. Double-O and I were so inseparable that people in the neighborhood called us by a single name: "Mike-n-Bond."

Meanwhile, my friendship with Tony and Greg was fraying at the edges. I was becoming one of the "cool kids." Our only contact was during three-way telephone prayer circles when Greg was in sickle cell crisis (which was becoming more frequent). Tony and Greg didn't play sports but they understood my Holy Ghost aspirations. James didn't own a single gospel mixtape and he referred to all comics as "cartoon books." When my junior high nerd circle reached high school, would I resume my puritanical ways or should I come out of the closet as a sinner? What would they think when they found out I owned a Run-DMC album called *Raising Hell*? Would they call me a blasphemer? I had to make a choice. No man could serve two Gods.

It all came to a head at the Twenty-Third Annual HYPU Youth Convention.

Every branch of the HOF had a youth group called the Holy Young People's Union. All year, each group paid dues, hosted events, and served as a support system for people under twenty-five who had given their life to Christ. At the end of every summer, all seven branches of the HOF convened for a weeklong youth summit with panel discussions, gospel jam sessions, and, of course, prayer. To explain our purpose for gathering, every session began with the HYPU theme song, which was, again, penned by its founder . . .

My mom.

> *We are the HYPU—Holy Young People's Union*
> *We are the HYPU—Holy Young People's Union*
> *We are here to serve the Lord and call upon his naaaame*
> *We are the HYPU—Holy Young People's Union**

The summer before my freshman year, the HYPU convention was in Hartsville, so naturally, James and I were required to attend. As we sat at the back of the church trying to holla at the semisanctified girls to see if we could catch them backsliding, my soul was in turmoil. I was pretending to be disinterested, but I was worried about the last day of the convention.

Because the location of the HYPU conventions alternated among the churches, it was the first time in seven years that Hartsville would host the event. Of course, Hartsville's HYPU chapter—the *founding chapter*—pulled out all the stops. On Saturday—the last and most-attended day of the convention—they scheduled a special guest speaker who was not in the HYPU but had become a viral legend in the youth Holy Ghost movement:

Gregory Prince.

All week, between dirt court basketball games and Jesus-focused plenary sessions, I fielded calls from Gregory Prince, who was so gripped with nervous fear about his keynote address that he went into crisis. Tony and I tried to comfort him but I also subtly let him know that he could cancel at any time. But Gregory had the Holy Ghost and he was a man of his word. He was determined to come.

That Friday, during the convention break, we were hanging in the church with some of the youth musicians from the other churches. As one of them played a nice shouting beat on the drums, James began playing a tune on the church piano. Everyone present had the Holy

---

* Y'all, I *swear* these are actual lyrics.

Ghost, so I was the only one who recognized that James was playing the melody from Boogie Down Productions' "Criminal Minded" . . . *at church!* It was one of the most egregious, brazen anti–Holy Ghost acts I had ever seen.

I was laughing slyly at Double-O when Elder Johnson walked in with my mother. They called me and James to the office and closed the door. It was about to go down. James was pretending to be confused but I could tell from the look in my mom's eyes that feigning innocence wouldn't work. The Holy Ghost leads and guides, so they knew we had defiled the sanctuary by playing the devil's music. Would I be formally excommunicated or was I about to be disinherited from the Harriot Holy Ghost? I had heard stories about God striking people dead for defiling His house and now I was going to feel it myself.

"Gregory Prince is in the hospital," they said. "He's in bad condition."

That's all?

I didn't tell them that Gregory Prince was in the hospital *all the time.* His family probably called to tell them he couldn't make it to the HYPU convention. I figured Tony was probably trying to call me for a prayer session, so I told everyone I was gonna go home. Everyone knew about our friendship so they understood, but Double-O had a better idea. He had just earned his driver's license and his granddaddy drove the church bus, so Double-O began corralling the future Holy Ghosters of America into the church van and we all drove to the hospital. We were gonna pray the sickle cell anemia off the legendary Gregory Prince!

When we arrived at the hospital, they wouldn't let all of these Black teenagers into a room. But Gregory's family was there, so they allowed me to visit. I had never visited Gregory *in the hospital,* so it looked pretty dire. He was in so much pain, he could barely talk. I was sitting awkwardly with Gregory's cussing daddy when Sister Wilene and Gregory's mother entered and opened the window. Outside, in the parking lot, the HYPU conventioneers began praying! They were summoning His divine healing, the miracle-working, the Grace of

God, the Holy Blessing, the sanctified power, the anointing . . . *All of the blessings.* They had a church service *in the parking lot.*

It might be blasphemy, but the only way to describe what they were doing:

They were praying like a motherfucker.

Apparently, Double-O was not the defiant unbeliever he portrayed himself to be. When I exited the building and hopped in Brother Jay's van, he plopped down beside me, sat shoulder to shoulder, and, without looking in my direction, whispered: "He's gon' be aight."

I didn't burst their bubble by telling him, or the HYPU varsity prayer team, that this was a regular occurrence with Gregory. Instead, I resolved to let the incident become part of the folklore of the magical Household of Faith Holy Ghost powers. On the ride back, I imagined that soon, the holiest people in South Carolina would be sharing the story of when Michael Harriot's fifth-generation superpowers healed a Holy Ghost legend.

Gregory Prince died later that night.

I felt like it was my responsibility to reveal the news to the standing-room-only crowd at the HYPU. My grandmother was there, along with both Dorothys. Gregory's mom and dad were even there. Then again, they are always there. They are members of the Household of Faith now. James stood beside me and Sister Wilene held down the door until I broke the news. It would probably be poignant to say the crowd was hushed when they heard what happened, but that's not how it went down. They broke into song and praise. Everybody started dancing (except James, of course).

That's when I caught the everlasting Holy Ghost.

Maybe it was Gregory's leftovers. Perhaps I always had it. I didn't step in the name of Jesus's love or even shimmy like a Nupe. I merely realized that, ultimately, I am the embodiment of my invisible ancestors' legacy. I am the substance of everything they have ever hoped for, the living, breathing evidence of things they have not seen. With nothing but their will to survive and the refusal to keep their mouths closed, they built a home that still stands and produced a miracle that is me.

I praise their holy names.

I will praise them in the sanctuary they built. I praise them in the firmament of their power. I praise them for their mighty acts and their excellent greatness. I praise them with the sound of my trumpet and the passion of my dance. Let everything that hath breath praise their sacred names.

Black people are a Holy Ghost . . .

Commandment keepers are we.

An Ode to Cappin'-Ass Niggas

✳

DAMON YOUNG

I t had to be 2004 or 2005. Because that's when I was dating Nicole. And watching *The Real World* on the living room couch at her mother's house was our second-favorite thing to do. And we were watching the segment on the first episode of a new season where they introduce each of the new characters with a montage filled with audition-tape B-roll of them doing the things they presumably do when they're not stuck in a house with seven strangers, seventeen crew members, and seventeen million viewers. And they introduced this Black guy named Karamo. And immediately Nicole was like, "Oh, he's cute." And immediately I was like, "Oh, he's gay." Which in the moment was just me hating. But I was on the right side of history. Anyway, his montage was mostly unmemorable in the way that these things are constructed to be. How many times can you watch a five-second clip of someone installing a carpet to exhibit their love of Jesus before it all becomes one amorphous wall of subtext? But then Karamo said and did something that will remain in my consciousness until I die. He described himself as "athletic." Which, okay, fine. He was in shape. He looked the part. He was muscular. I could have whooped his ass, but it would have been a struggle. But then they showed him shooting a layup at an outdoor basketball court and catching the ball out of the net and this nigga looked like he'd never touched a basketball before in his life. He shot it like it was a loaf of bread. And not a full loaf either, but a loaf that had been cut into twenty slices and would crumble if he held it funny. Can a shot attempt be gluten-free? Don't answer that. Just know that he caught it out of the net like someone just threw a roll of toilet paper down a flight of stairs to him. He caught it like it was a baby. Not his baby though. Not even a baby he had a tangential connection to or affinity for. But a random baby someone just decided to throw at him. I mean, imagine for a second what you would do if you were walking down the street and someone was like, "Catch!" and you were expecting a football or a watermelon or COVID but instead it was a baby. How awkward would that be for you? How confused would you be while that baby was midair? How invested would you be in the series of decisions that led to a baby being thrown at you? How many questions would you have about chance and serendipity and child protective services? That was how that nigga looked. It was my duty as a basketball snob to hate Karamo for that lie. And so I did for a while. But then the hate dissipated into a curiosity. (Was that his idea? Did they ask him to do it? Why did he agree to do it? Why did they air that footage?) And then the curiosity transmuted into an appreciation for the grift. It didn't matter anymore whose idea it was. What mattered instead was Karamo's commitment to the bit. He knew he couldn't hoop. But he also had to know that a young and athletic-looking Black man is expected to at least have a cursory competency on the hoop court and that none of the white people in the production room would question why he hooped like the ball was a box of Frosted Flakes. He also had lived experience as a queer Black man, so of course he had a relationship with the concept of performance. The idea of faking it till you make it. The reality that sometimes it's necessary to send a representative. All lies ain't created equal, of course. Some lies shame. Some lies kill. Some lies convince us to invade Iraq. But then you have the embellishments. The hyperbole. The exaggerations that don't really harm anyone. It's the difference between a lie that you slept with a real-life woman whom you know but had never actually been with and Wilt Chamberlain's claim to have boned twenty thousand women. One has real-world reputational consequences. The other has none and exists solely to verify audacity and conjure debate about its veracity. I grew up on these lies. My dad had five brothers. All athletes. All cads. All storytellers. All liars. Who entertained us with claims about middle school football touchdown records and flaccid-dick-size estimates of rumored-to-be-well-endowed garbagemen and highway Frisbee sessions with Charlie No-Face—shit that could and would only be verified by them. My cousins and I would gather each summer on porches and in living rooms in New Castle at my grandma's and my aunt Elener's or in Youngstown at my aunt Jean's, and we'd plot our entire years around the privilege of soaking up these stories. We knew these niggas were capping because they'd tell them each summer and the details would change each time. But we loved it and we loved them and we loved them for it. I think we were beginning to realize even then the virtuosic value of a capping-ass nigga. And I'm not saying that Black men specifically are the only people who lie. We ain't the most prolific or destructive (white men) or even really the best at it (white women). But there's a flourish and a tenacity and an entertainment value to the capping-ass nigga that is singular. These lies have roots, of course, in the necessity of armor-building and protecting us and who we love from *them*. I'm reminded specifically of *The Hateful Eight* and how the fabricated letter from Lincoln that Sam Jackson always kept in his breast pocket saved his life more times than he probably cared to count. I mean, what is being Black and male and American more than selling a lifesaving lie so hard that you're sure a nigga will never call your bluff? But then it also exists within the tradition of oral storytelling. How we communicated to each other and with each other at the both the highest and the lowest possible frequencies. It's forty-two-year-old Pusha T twenty-five years into his rap career reminding us that seventeen-year-old him sold enough coke to "predict the snow" like "Al Roker" when we know that nigga's lying but appreciate the methodological rigor of the fantasy he's selling us. I know that Katt Williams has never and could never run forty yards in 4.2 seconds as he claimed to be able to do while on a podcast with Shannon Sharpe. But the point isn't that he's capping or that he's delusional or that he's drunk or even to watch him run and note that he moves like a five-year-old trying on new shoes. No, the point is to ask yourself if you'd dare race him.

Group Chat

DEESHA PHILYAW

*Mama (*THAT LADY*) texts the group chat she shares with her daughters, Ayana (*YANA BANA*) and* MONIQUE*.*

THAT LADY
I think I just killed your father.

YANA BANA
OMG WHAT

MONIQUE
FINALLY
Kidding!
Ma, an "LOL" from you would be real helpful right now . . .

YANA BANA
What happened???????

MONIQUE
Wait! Don't reply, Ma!
Text messages are admissible as evidence in court.
Although . . . 53 years is a long time to put up with bullshit.
I think a jury of at least 50% women would refuse to convict.
Call me, Ma.

THAT LADY

Don't say bullshit. I keep shaking him and calling his name but he won't wake up. Father God!

YANA BANA

Why should she call you? Because you failed the LSAT 15 years ago? Mama, I'm calling 911.

THAT LADY

No!

YANA BANA

Then I'm calling you.

MONIQUE

Call me on 3-way!

YANA BANA

Mama, pick up!
OMG, Mo, it's a murder-suicide! We're orphans!

THAT LADY

Girl, calm down! I ain't dead. I just don't feel like talking right now.

YANA BANA

You killed Daddy, I think we need to talk! I'm calling 911.

THAT LADY

I said no!

MONIQUE

I'm sure she didn't kill Daddy. Sounds like she's simply in a distressed state. Not unlike a person experiencing a psychotic break after years of trauma, one who cannot be held culpable for her actions while in said state.

YANA BANA

Watching every episode of *Criminal Minds* and *Law & Order* twice doesn't make you an expert.

THAT LADY
  (typing)

MONIQUE
  Expert deez

YANA BANA
  Really? Are you 12?

MONIQUE
  Ma, is Daddy breathing?

THAT LADY
  Hold on. Let me check.
    Yeah. He's breathing.

YANA BANA
  Oh thank God!

THAT LADY
  I have a question. But I need y'all to promise me y'all gonna take this to the grave.

MONIQUE
  Promise

YANA BANA
  I'm coming over right now.

THAT LADY
  No!

MONIQUE
  For fuck's sake, Yana! Just promise!

THAT LADY
  Language!

MONIQUE
  Sorry, Ma.

YANA BANA

> Don't cuss at me! I wouldn't even be talking to you if Mama hadn't texted.

THAT LADY

> Are y'all fighting again?

MONIQUE

> No, ma'am.

YANA BANA

> Yes, ma'am!

MONIQUE

> She just mad because I don't want her old bed.

YANA BANA

> No, I'm mad because you said you wanted the bed, then changed your mind, and now I have to find someone at the last minute and pay them to haul it away before I have to vacate my apartment on Friday.

MONIQUE

> Why don't you just take the bed to your new place?

Ayana to Monique only

YANA BANA

> Because it's got the ghost of Andrew's dick all up in it, and I'm not bringing that into my next chapter.

MONIQUE

> Just sage it to clear the disappointing dick energy, duh. And then palo santo the whole apt. #solved
> You know what's really fucked up?

YANA BANA

> The fact that you never keep your word?

MONIQUE

The fact that we wouldn't be clowning like this if Daddy had texted us that he'd just killed Mama.

YANA BANA

This family circus only has one clown and it's not me . . .

MONIQUE

Yeah, it's ya daddy.

In the group chat

THAT LADY

Ayana Michelle . . . promise!

YANA BANA

Ok ok I promise. But with all due respect, if you don't put Daddy on the phone in 5 minutes, I'm calling 911.

MONIQUE

Can you chill, please!?

Ma, you said you had a question . . .

THAT LADY

(typing)

YANA BANA

Don't you tell me to chill when our father is in peril!

MONIQUE

Ok, Guinevere 😎

YANA BANA

I can't believe you're using emojis at a time like this.

THAT LADY

(typing)

THAT LADY

Ok. You know when you . . . a man's . . . does it . . . is it supposed to. You know.

YANA BANA

Mama, are you having a stroke? Go look in the mirror. Is your mouth crooked?

MONIQUE

She's not having a stroke, fool.

Ma, start from the beginning. What happened? Did Daddy fall or hit his head?

YANA BANA

If he fell or hit his head, why would she say she killed him, Jessica Fletcher?

THAT LADY

No, he didn't fall or nothing. But come to think of it, he did have a few dranks before we went to bed.

MONIQUE

We're talking about Daddy here. "A few dranks" usually means half a fifth of Jack. Can you be more specific?

Hol' up. It ain't but 6:30 now. What time did y'all go to bed???

YANA BANA

Yeah that is early . . . Was Daddy not feeling well?

THAT LADY

No, he was feeling just fine. This was his idea.

YANA BANA

What was his idea?

MONIQUE

What was his idea?

THAT LADY

Well, the pill was his idea. That other thing . . . I was just curious is all, Lord forgive me.

MONIQUE
> What pill???

YANA BANA
> What pill???

THAT LADY
> A little blue one

Ayana to Monique only

YANA BANA
> OMGOMGOMGOMGOMG

MONIQUE
> LMAO

YANA BANA
> I need some brain bleach. Like, right now.

MONIQUE
> Because Mama and Daddy had sex?

YANA BANA
> Because they are STILL having sex! Why??

MONIQUE
> Why not? Don't you want to still be fucking in your 70s?

In the group chat

THAT LADY
> Hello?

YANA BANA
> No, I do not want to still be fucking in my 70s!

MONIQUE
> Wrong chat . . .

THAT LADY

What? Hello?

YANA BANA

Oh damn!

MONIQUE

Language!

THAT LADY

He only took the one pill. I thought it was supposed to keep him . . . not knock him out. You think he shoulda just taken half of one?

Ayana to Monique only

YANA BANA

Answer her. Surely as a graduate of *Grey's Anatomy* University, you got something.

In the group chat

MONIQUE

He'll be fine, Ma. Just let him sleep it off.

THAT LADY

So this is what happens when you . . . you know.

MONIQUE

Take Viagra?

THAT LADY

No . . . I did something.

Ayana to Monique only

YANA BANA

I'm about to throw my phone out the window and throw up my guts.

In the group chat

THAT LADY

Remember long time ago what I told y'all only dirty white girls do? Well, I did it, and I think it knocked ya Daddy out cold.

MONIQUE

Ohhhhhhh. Ok. Nah. He's fine, Ma. You sucked the soul out his dick is all.

Ayana to Monique only

YANA BANA

I really hate you.

In the group chat

THAT LADY

Language!

MONIQUE

Sorry

YANA BANA

Shouldn't she turn him over on his stomach, so if he vomits he won't choke and die?

MONIQUE

If she moves him that could complicate an investigation. Just stay in the guest room, Ma. And try to get some sleep. I'll come by in the morning.

YANA BANA

I will come by even earlier in the morning. Good night, Mama.

MONIQUE

Good night, Ma. Good night, weird, ridiculously competitive sister.

THAT LADY
> Good night, girls.

Monique to Ayana only

MONIQUE
> Ain't that a bitch? After all the things that trifling man has put
> her through, he has the nerve to ask her to give him head!

YANA BANA
> She said it was her idea. Sounds like she offered.
>> OMG you really are a witch. I can't believe I just typed that!

In the group chat

THAT LADY
> Love you.

MONIQUE
> Trust, if I was a witch, I would've helped Mama kill his ass
> a long time ago and left not a trace. She'd be on an island
> somewhere living off his insurance money and pension right
> now.

YANA BANA
> Wrong chat, Annalise Keating!

MONIQUE
> Just kidding, Mama! HAHAHA LOLOLOL

Monique to Ayana only

MONIQUE
> SHIT

YANA BANA
> Stop texting. I'm calling you.

"Hey. It's okay," Yana says. "I think she went to bed."

"She's going to see it when she wakes up."

"Not if you delete it right now."

"Hold on . . . ," Monique says. "Done. Anyway. Can you believe this shit? She's worrying about his pleasure. What about hers? When has he ever thought about what Mama wants, what Mama needs? How many forgotten birthdays and anniversaries is she supposed to put up with? How many lies? How many other women? How many times are y'all going to have to get him out of the drunk tank?"

"It's called a sobering cell. And alcoholism is a disease."

"Yes, and there is treatment. But Daddy isn't interested in it. Mama shouldn't have to keep suffering because he refuses to get help."

"How do you know she's suffering?"

"Would you be happy in her position?"

"She told me she made vows, and she intends to keep them. In sickness and in health. Till death do us part."

"I'm familiar with the vows . . ."

"But you don't think keeping them is important. Because you don't believe in marriage as an institution."

"You made air quotes when you said 'institution,' didn't you?"

"Maybe."

"I don't believe marriage should be a prison for women," Monique says. "And it's always women who are expected to keep the vows, come hell or high water. Let Mama have done a fraction of the things Daddy's done, and he would've been out. If she had stepped out on him even once, he would've bounced, and you know it."

Yana sighs.

"Well, this is now heavy as fuck," Monique says. "Good thing my edible should be kicking in any minute now."

"Of course you're high . . . All I'm saying is I understand wanting to keep your word, when it's someone you care about."

Silence.

"Are we still talking about Mama and Daddy?" Monique asks.

"You tell me. And for the record, I would not be happy in Mama's position. Why do you think I kicked Andrew to the curb?"

Again, silence.

"What?" Yana says.

"This is me refraining from saying something rude but absolutely hilarious."

"Go ahead. Say it."

"You kicked Andrew to the curb because he's also an alcoholic with wack peen?"

"No! . . . Well, the wack peen part is true. But that's not the main reason. The main reason is I do plan to keep my vows and be married forever. But I realized Andrew is not 'forever' material."

"He really isn't. I don't even know what that means, but I know he isn't."

"What I mean is he's completely unmotivated and stagnant. It would've been more like living with a dependent than a life partner."

"And I know you not trying to take in a foster man. Yeah, I feel you, Yana Yana Bo Bana Fee Fi Mo Nana."

"The edible kick in?"

"Yep," Monique says, popping the P hard.

"Bye."

"So in closing, what did we learn tonight, kids? Besides the fact that our father hasn't had a blow job in over fifty years?"

"I said BYE!"

"Yana?"

"What!?"

"Yana?"

"WHAT?"

"Let me find out your mama is the throat GOAT."

"GOODBYE!"

"Yana?"

"Monique, please go rewatch NCIS and stop playing on my phone."

"I'll call 1-800-JUNK and have them haul your old bed away. My treat."

"Is that you or the edible talking?"

"We shall see. We shall see."

From: Todd ▮▮▮▮▮▮▮▮▮▮
To: Damon Young ▮▮▮▮▮▮▮▮▮▮▮
Subject: Racism Is Really Bad

Good afternoon, good sir!

I really enjoyed "Racism Is Really Bad"—your expert deconstruction of racism, race as a social construct instead of the biological certainty it's believed to be, and privilege; especially how you articulated its historical and present-day connections and interlinkages to all aspects of American life. I never quite understood how it resonates on both a literal and metaphysical level, and your piece really drove that home, contextualizing everything down to even the most minute distinctions.

Racism generally and the treatment of displaced Africans specifically is our national disgrace, a shame both literal and existential, and your examination of this sickness was brave, blunt, and necessary. There is no piece of literature existing today that is more pertinent, prescient, and relevant, and I am proud to call you my countryman, my neighbor, and perhaps, if you bestow the honor, my friend.

Also, you're a nigger.

Best,
Todd

Acknowledgments

I am forever indebted to my family for lifting me up, my friends for sitting me down, and everyone who impacted the construction of this book and the messy ingenuity inside it. Including everyone at McKinnon Literary and Pantheon Books for indulging my circus of chaotic neuroses, the University of Pittsburgh's Frederick Honors College and the City of Asylum for making space for me to be, the twenty-four generous geniuses who trusted me enough to allow me to convince them to be in this, and the tens of millions of Black Americans who've inspired me through the bottomless cultural alchemy that existing while *us* necessitates. It is an honor to feel and to be felt by them.

Also, in my household growing up, my dad was the Anointer, which means that if a movie or a show or even just a story made him laugh, it meant that the effort to be funny had surpassed garden-variety humor and ascended to something transcendent, visceral, and even ethereal. I like to pretend that I possess that status in my household now, that I'm the nigga with the most refined comedic sensibility. But unfortunately (for me) that title belongs to my son, who at the time of writing is six years old and withholds laughs at my jokes like he's rationing them in exchange for hours on the iPad.

If anything in this book makes either of them laugh, mission accomplished.

About the Contributors

HANIF ABDURRAQIB is a poet, essayist, and cultural critic from Columbus, Ohio. He is the author of the National Book Award finalist *A Little Devil in America;* the *New York Times* bestseller *Go Ahead in the Rain: Notes to a Tribe Called Quest,* which was a finalist for the National Book Critics Circle Award and the Kirkus Prize; the poetry collection *The Crown Ain't Worth Much;* and the highly acclaimed essay collection *They Can't Kill Us Until They Kill Us.* His work has appeared in *Muzzle, Vinyl, PEN America, Pitchfork, The New Yorker,* and *The New York Times.*

MATEO ASKARIPOUR wants people to feel seen. His first novel, *Black Buck,* takes on racism in corporate America with humor and wit. It was an instant *New York Times* bestseller and a Read with Jenna *Today* show book club pick. Askaripour was chosen as one of *Entertainment Weekly's* "10 rising stars poised to make waves" and was named as a recipient of the National Book Foundation's "5 Under 35" prize. *This Great Hemisphere* is his second novel. He lives in Brooklyn.

BRIAN BROOME's debut memoir, *Punch Me Up to the Gods,* is a *New York Times* Editors' Pick and the winner of the 2021 Kirkus Prize for nonfiction. He is a contributing columnist at *The Washington Post.* His work has also appeared in *Hippocampus, Poets & Writers, Medium,* and more. Broome was a K. Leroy Irvis Fellow. He has been a finalist in The Moth storytelling competition and won the grand prize in Carnegie Mellon University's Martin Luther King, Jr. Day Writing Awards. Broome also won a Robert L. Vann Media Award from the Pittsburgh Black Media Federation for journalism in 2019. His film, *Garbage,* won the Audience Choice Award at the Mirada Cortada Short Film Festival and was a semifinalist in the Portland Short Fest.

MAHOGANY L. BROWNE, a Kennedy Center's Next 50 fellow and Mac-Dowell Arts Advocacy awardee, is a writer, playwright, organizer, and educator. Browne received fellowships from All Arts, Art for Justice, AIR Serenbe, Baldwin for the Arts, Cave Canem, Hawthornden, Poets House, the Mellon Foundation, Rauschenberg, Wesleyan University, and Ucross. Browne's books include *Vinyl Moon, Chlorine Sky* (optioned for a play by Steppenwolf Theatre), *Black Girl Magic,* and banned books *Woke: A Young Poet's Call to Justice* and *Woke Baby.* Founder of the diverse lit initiative Woke Baby Book Fair, Browne currently tours *Chrome Valley* (highlighted in *Publishers Weekly* and *The New York Times*) and is the 2024 Paterson Poetry Prize winner. Browne holds an honorary Doctor of Philosophy degree awarded by Marymount Manhattan College and is the inaugural poet-in-residence at Lincoln Center.

JILL LOUISE BUSBY is a writer and filmmaker critiquing, imploding, and barrel-laughing at our personal and communal hierarchies; the endlessly pending and highly exclusive revolution, identity, reaction, and our grandest illusions; and the boundaries that they all place on our lives. Busby's work charms audiences just past their limits of comfort, inviting them to seek a new and more genuine freedom in the discomfort of truth. She is the author of *Unfollow Me: Essays on Complicity* (Bloomsbury, 2021).

WYATT CENAC is an Emmy Award–winning comedian known for the HBO late-night comedy docuseries *Wyatt Cenac's Problem Areas.* Additional credits include *aka Wyatt Cenac, People of Earth,* and *The Daily Show.* He's released four stand-up albums; his 2014 album and

Netflix special, *Wyatt Cenac: Brooklyn,* was nominated for a Grammy. Cenac was a writer for Mike Judge's *King of the Hill,* served as a consultant for *South Park,* and wrote an animated musical starring Steve Urkel . . . Yes, that Steve Urkel. Every now and again he pops up in a film, most notably Barry Jenkins's *Medicine for Melancholy.*

ASHON CRAWLEY is professor of religious studies and African American and African studies at the University of Virginia. He is the author of *Blackpentecostal Breath: The Aesthetics of Possibility* (2016) and *The Lonely Letters* (2020). An artist, his audiovisual art has been featured at Second Street Gallery, Bridge Projects, the California African American Museum, and the National Mall in Washington, DC. All his work is about otherwise possibility.

HILLARY CROSLEY COKER is a New York–based journalist, editor, and producer with over twenty years covering entertainment, politics, and culture. You can find her at @HillaryCrosley on Twitter until The Man ruins it for good. She loves black tea, her Black family, sarcastic jokes, and British television—she knows that last one is problematic, but even her conditioning has been conditioned. Cheers, mate!

SAIDA GRUNDY is the author of *Respectable: Politics and Paradox in Making the Morehouse Man.* She is a feminist sociologist of race and ethnicity and an associate professor of sociology, African American and Black diaspora studies, and women's and gender studies at Boston University. A proud graduate of Spelman College, she received her PhD in sociology and women's studies from the University of Michigan and often contributes to *The Atlantic.*

ALEXANDER HARDY is a grits-powered writer, Mental Health First Aid National Trainer, home cook, and lupus survivor. He will probably ask what delicious meals you've eaten recently. Hardy battles spiritual ashiness as co-founder of GetSomeJoy, a creative wellness agency, and is on a lifelong quest to make better empanadas. In 2022, after his mother died, he curated, designed, and published *griefKit:*

Tools and considerations for raggedy times as a creative wellness resource for GetSomeJoy. Hardy does not believe in snow or Delaware.

MICHAEL HARRIOT is an economist, a poet, and the author of the *New York Times* bestseller *Black AF History: The Un-Whitewashed Story of America*. An award-winning journalist and screenwriter, Harriot currently serves as the founder and executive editor of Contraband-Camp, a digital media collective.

CLOVER HOPE is an acclaimed journalist whose writing has appeared in the pages of *Vibe, Vogue, Esquire, Essence, Elle, GQ, Wall Street Journal Magazine, The New York Times, Cosmopolitan, Wired, ESPN,* and *Billboard,* among others. Prior to going freelance, Hope worked as a staff writer and editor at *Billboard, XXL, Vibe,* and *Jezebel.* She's currently an NYU professor and creative consultant whose notable productions include Beyoncé's Emmy-winning visual film *Black Is King* (2021) and the Hulu docuseries *RapCaviar Presents* (2023). Her book, *The Motherlode: 100+ Women Who Made Hip-Hop,* is a comprehensive, illustrated history of women in hip-hop, available in bookstores and as an Audible Originals audiobook.

SHAMIRA IBRAHIM is a Brooklyn-based culture writer by way of Harlem, Canada, and East Africa who explores identity and cultural production as a critic, reporter, feature/profile writer, and essayist. Her work has been featured in publications such as *New York* magazine, *Essence, The Atlantic, The New York Times, The Washington Post, Teen Vogue, BuzzFeed, Vox, OkayAfrica, The Root, Mic, The Baffler,* and *Harper's Bazaar.*

PANAMA JACKSON is an award-winning writer, author, and columnist for theGrio.com and host of the *Dear Culture* podcast on theGrio Black Podcast Network. Because he believes the children are our future, he is also an adjunct lecturer at Howard University. He is co-founder and former senior editor of the award-winning website VerySmartBrothas.com, cited as "the blackest place on the internet" by *The Washington Post.* He graduated from Morehouse College with a degree in economics and holds a master's degree in public policy from the University of Maryland, College Park, and *really* enjoys getting paid to be Black for a living.

KIESE LAYMON is a Black southern writer from Jackson, Mississippi.

ANGELA NISSEL writes books and TV shows, and started an award-winning music website, but really just enjoys her rescue pitbull and eating overpriced fancy donuts.

LADAN OSMAN is the author of *Exiles of Eden* (2019), winner of a Whiting Award and the Hurston/Wright Legacy Award, and *The Kitchen-Dweller's Testimony* (2015), winner of the Sillerman Prize. Her work in film includes *The Ascendants; Sam, Underground;* and *Sun of the Soil.* She lives in New York.

DEESHA PHILYAW's debut short story collection, *The Secret Lives of Church Ladies,* won the 2021 PEN/Faulkner Award for Fiction, the 2020/2021 Story Prize, and the 2020 Los Angeles Times Book Prize's Art Seidenbaum Award for First Fiction, and was a finalist for the 2020 National Book Award for Fiction. Her debut novel, *The True Confessions of First Lady Freeman,* is forthcoming from Mariner Books, an imprint of HarperCollins, in 2026.

RION AMILCAR SCOTT is the author of the story collections *The World Doesn't Require You* and *Insurrections,* which was awarded the 2017 PEN/Bingham Prize for Debut Fiction and the 2017 Hillsdale Award from the Fellowship of Southern Writers. He teaches creative writing at the University of Maryland, College Park. His work has appeared in *The New Yorker, The Kenyon Review, The Best American Science Fiction and Fantasy 2020,* and *McSweeney's Quarterly Concern,* among other publications.

JOSEPH EARL THOMAS is the author of the memoir *Sink,* which was longlisted for the PEN/Jean Stein Book Award; the novel *God Bless You, Otis Spunkmeyer;* and the forthcoming story collection *Levia-*

than Beach. His writing has been published in *The Kenyon Review, The Paris Review, Virginia Quarterly Review, Dilettante Army,* and *The New York Times Book Review.* He is a graduate of the University of Notre Dame's MFA program in prose and holds a PhD in English from the University of Pennsylvania.

NAFISSA THOMPSON-SPIRES is the author of *Heads of the Colored People,* which won the PEN Open Book Award, the Hurston/Wright Award for Fiction, and the Los Angeles Times Book Prize's Art Seidenbaum Award for First Fiction. Her collection was longlisted for the National Book Award, the PEN/Robert W. Bingham Prize, and several other prizes, including an NAACP Image Award. She is also the recipient of a 2019 Whiting Award. She earned a doctorate in English from Vanderbilt University and a master's of fine arts in creative writing from the University of Illinois. With dark humor, covering topics from identity to chronic illness, her short fiction and essays have appeared in *The Paris Review*'s The Daily, *New York* magazine's The Cut, *The Root, The White Review, Ploughshares, 400 Souls: A Community History of African America, 1619–2019,* and *The 1619 Project,* among other publications. In addition to a forthcoming novel from Scribner, she has new writing in *Fourteen Days: A Community Gathering,* edited by Margaret Atwood. She is the 2024 winner of a United States Artists Grant.

D WATKINS is the *New York Times* bestselling author of *The Beast Side, The Cook Up, Where Tomorrows Aren't Promised, Black Boy Smile,* and other books. His book *We Speak for Ourselves* was Enoch Pratt Free Library's 2020 One Book Baltimore selection. Some of Watkins's awards include the James Beard Media Award, Gordon Parks Foundation Fellowship, Enoch Pratt Free Library's Hackerman Writer in Residence, Vernon Jarrett Medal for Journalistic Excellence, Society of Professional Journalists Dateline Award for Commentary, Gold Signal Award, Johns Hopkins University Society of Scholars, Johns Hopkins University Distinguished Alumnus Award, CityLit's Dambach Award for Service to the Literary Arts, and the Maryland Library Association's William G. Wilson Maryland Author Award. Watkins is editor-at-large for *Salon.* Additionally, he is a writer on the

HBO miniseries *We Own This City* and host of the show's companion podcast. He was also featured in the HBO documentary *The Slow Hustle*. His work has been published in *The New York Times, Esquire, The New York Times Magazine, The Guardian, Rolling Stone,* and other publications. Watkins is a professor at the University of Baltimore, where he earned a bachelor's of arts in history and a master's of fine arts in creative writing. He also holds a master's of education from Johns Hopkins University.

ROY WOOD JR., host of CNN's *Have I Got News for You,* is a comedian, an Emmy-nominated documentary producer for the PBS documentary *The Neutral Ground,* a former correspondent and guest host on Comedy Central's Emmy-nominated *The Daily Show,* and, in 2023, he headlined the White House Correspondents' Dinner. He has appeared on *Late Night with Seth Meyers, Conan, The Tonight Show Starring Jimmy Fallon, The Late Show with Stephen Colbert, Last Week Tonight with John Oliver, Only Murders in the Building,* and *Better Call Saul.*

NICOLA YOON is the number one *New York Times* bestselling author of *Instructions for Dancing; Everything, Everything; The Sun Is Also a Star;* and *One of Our Kind,* and a co-author of *Blackout* and *Whiteout.* She is a National Book Award finalist, a Michael L. Printz Honor Book recipient, and a John Steptoe Award for New Talent winner. Two of her novels have been made into major motion pictures. She's also the co-publisher of Joy Revolution, a Random House young adult imprint dedicated to love stories starring people of color. She grew up in Jamaica and Brooklyn and lives in Los Angeles with her husband, the novelist David Yoon, and their daughter.

ABOUT THE EDITOR

Pittsburgh writer Damon Young's debut memoir, *What Doesn't Kill You Makes You Blacker: A Memoir in Essays* (Ecco), won the Thurber Prize for American Humor. Young is also a founder of the culture blog *Very Smart Brothas* and was a contributing columnist for *The Washington Post Magazine*, a contributing opinion writer for *The New York Times*, a columnist for *GQ*, and the creator and host of the Crooked Media podcast *Stuck with Damon Young*. Currently, he is the inaugural writer-in-residence at the University of Pittsburgh's David C. Frederick Honors College.

A NOTE ON THE TYPE

This book was set in Monotype Dante, a typeface designed by Giovanni Mardersteig (1892–1977). Conceived as a private type for the Officina Bodoni in Verona, Italy, Dante was originally cut for hand composition by Charles Malin, the famous Parisian punch cutter, between 1946 and 1952. Its first use was in an edition of Boccaccio's *Trattatello in laude di Dante* that appeared in 1954. The Monotype Corporation's version of Dante followed in 1957. Although modeled on the Aldine type used for Pietro Cardinal Bembo's treatise *De Aetna* in 1495, Dante is a thoroughly modern interpretation of the venerable face.

Typeset by Scribe,
Philadelphia, Pennsylvania

Designed by Cassandra J. Pappas